DATE DUE

DEMCO 38-296

VS Hixson

"Actually, I liked the students I used to get at the
Community College better than the ones I get here at the
university, but for God's sake, don't tell anybody I
said that."

CONTENTS

Contents

INTRODUCTION

Joseph N. Hankin

The Sunday edition of a large metropolitan newspaper like the *New York Times* might contain as many as a half-million words. To complete reading every page, at an average reading speed of 300 words per minute, would take more than one full day of reading, every minute of every hour. According to Patricia Glass Schuman in the March 1, 1990, *Library Journal,* a weekly edition of the same newspaper contains more information than the average person was likely to come across in a lifetime in seventeenth-century England (35).

How to cope with this surfeit of information has become the challenge of twentieth-century educational institutions and their libraries. We have collected in them the words of learned men and women and the sounds of rock bands. The Northwestern University Dental School Library has a collection of Tooth Fairy artifacts, including coins and pillows. The Plainedge (N.Y.) Public Library offers patrons gardening and woodworking tools, sewing machines, and floor buffers. Others lend out paintings, dress patterns, and even gerbils. It will not be long before our libraries will capture not just the sights and sounds of current-day life, but the tastes and smells will also be preserved for our children and grandchildren.

Gone is the time (if it ever existed) when Ring Lardner could say, "Mr. [Irvin] Cobb took me into his library and showed me his books, of which he has a complete set." There will be no such thing as a "complete set" of anything. Even a large institution like the Library of Congress, which receives one thousand new titles daily, cannot ever possibly plan to acquire everything.

The authors represented in this volume come from many

sections of this country and Canada, and from different settings—urban, rural, suburban. They address themselves to the many increasingly complex issues facing the professional today. Librarians are more than their titles indicate, for they are working, productive, omnipresent members of the faculties of the institutions they represent. They are the vanguard of the consummate professionals others in the same occupation must be if they are to cope with the changes all about us and in the years ahead of us.

They are painfully aware that the use of the library has always been, and will continue to be, a reflection on the faculty as a whole and on the curriculum of their respective institutions. If, as Ernest Boyer reports, one of four undergraduates spends no time in the library during a normal week, and two-thirds use it fewer than four hours a week (Breivik and Wedgeworth 7), the librarians know that it is more than their fault. If a faculty member on campus is not aware that the periodicals section of the library changed its location two years ago, how can he or she expect students to make use of the library in a consistent manner, or prepare to make use of it for a lifetime of learning?

Finally, these librarian-professionals are very much aware, as each of them writes of excellence from a different point of view, that the excellence of a circle lies in its roundness, not in its bigness. Similarly, the excellence of the libraries of the future will rest on committed professionals like the authors and the readers who find the ideas presented herein not just acceptable, but ideas to be implemented. The Online Computer Library Center (OCLC) in Ohio now makes available to its members the catalog of the British Library. The day may not be too distant when students in your libraries will use their computers to read the catalog of any library in the world.

If synergism may be defined as "that which makes the whole greater than the sum of its parts," then this book and the libraries it describes will bring not just access but also excellence to our mutual task—preservation and expansion of the heritage of humanity.

Works Cited

Breivik, Patricia Senn, and Robert Wedgeworth, eds. *Libraries and the Search for Academic Excellence.* Metuchen, N.J.: Scarecrow, 1988.

Schuman, Patricia Glass. "Reclaiming Our Technological Future." *Library Journal* 1 Mar. 1990: 34–38.

PATTERNS OF EXCELLENCE

Rosanne Kalick

In less than 60 years, community colleges have grown from modest beginnings to an enrollment of more than 5.3 million students. This figure should rise to more than 6 million by the end of the century. John Gardner called the community college "the greatest educational invention of the 20th century" ("Academia's" 84), an invention Thomas Jefferson may have envisioned when he called for the creation of a college within one-day's travel for all Virginians (Hisle 614).

In 1936, the typical junior college library could seat 73 readers, had 5,618 books, an annual budget of $1,853, an average expenditure of $8.29 per student, for a total of 7.7% of the institution's budget (Eells 202). By 1958, junior college libraries averaged 10,454 books, but library expenditures were down to 3.5% of the college budget (Bock 38). The concept of learning resources was already established, the first audiovisual course having been taught by Louis Shores in 1935 (Hisle 617). Legitimacy was given to the term "learning resource center" when it was used in 1967 at a conference entitled "Junior College Libraries: Development, Needs, and Perspectives" (Bock 41).

What has this growth meant for the community college library? What does it portend for the future? Evan Farber suggests we must know "the politics of the institution, the purpose of the institution, the personnel of the institution, to know it well, to know its history" (Riggs 116). What is the library mission? How does it reflect the college mission? Indeed, every activity, program, policy in the learning resource center (library) should reflect in some manner the college mission, and librarians must serve as facilitators in the achievement of that mission. An examination of the community college library—whether it be called a learning resource center or a library—reveals patterns, patterns we can emulate or redesign to meet our particular college's needs. Those designs may enable us to create patterns of excellence which will make our libraries truly the educational center of the campus.

We must question if we are to create excellence. How can the community college library meet the educational needs of its users? What is the role of the library in terms of the community? What strategies can libraries use as they compete for limited college resources? How can librarians learn to communicate more effectively with the faculty and administration to meet the needs of its learners? How do we work with today's non-traditional community college student? What assessment tools are available to measure the library's role in the teaching/learning process? In other words, what questions must community college librarians ask and answer if they are to seek excellence?

There are no simple answers. What does seem clear, however, is that life in a community college in general and in the library in particular is one of change, contrasts, and activity. The better the library is able to respond to change, the more likely it will be able to meet the varied needs of its constituencies. Drake says we must "adopt, adapt, and innovate" (521) if we are to respond to today's challenges.

Developing a Climate of Excellence

Our goal is to help the student to function independently and successfully in an information-laden world. The focus, therefore, must be on the teaching/learning process. All library activities must be spokes in the wheel of lifelong learning. An appropriate library climate is essential if learning is to take place. With such a climate, the library should function well, and excitement, activity, and excellence result.

There are patterns of excellence in our community college libraries that make them centers of learning, centers of challenge, centers of innovation and change. To paraphrase Tom Peters, our libraries thrive on chaos. To work toward excellence, let us examine some of the activities, programs, and policies that create the best climate for learning. By doing so,

we may be able to extrapolate and select those elements that
we can use to make our own libraries more successful, and
enable us all to advance toward the goal of library excellence.
While reference and bibliographic instruction activities are
obviously part of the teaching/learning process, the role of
those in technical services, while less visible, is equally important. With more than 45,000 book titles published in America
annually, selective acquisition is critical. Librarians must use
traditional and non-traditional selection tools. Catalogers,
especially in the world of the on-line catalog, have pivotal
roles to play. The more information they enter during the
cataloging process, for example, the more likely it is that the
user will be able to browse and interact with the bibliographic
data, to engage in serendipitous research. The user who can
see the table of contents on-line as part of the bibliographic
record is helped in the process. Inaccessible or inappropriate
resources may not only impede the learning process; they
may sabotage it.

Teaching/Learning

The single most important element in the effort to achieve
excellence is the librarian. Ortega y Gasset in 1934 defined
the librarian as a filter interposed between people and the
"torrent" of books (Asheim 215); how much larger is the
torrent of information today! Asheim speaks of the librarian
as more than a selector; the librarian is not only the builder of
the store of information, but also the "intermediary between
that store and the user's present need" (219). Ernest Boyer
speaks of connectivity, suggesting that those in charge of
information be "renaissance" people who guide students as
they discover relationships that "no single department and no
single professor can provide" (Breivik and Wedgeworth *Libraries* 10). The most important concept then is that the
librarian claim a role in the teaching/learning process. Major
Owens speaks of the library as a salon where aesthetic standards and intellectual values can be set, where the benefits of
information literacy can be reaped, where learners can feast
on a "general information smorgasbord"; he describes the
library as a "well-placed watch-tower overlooking our global

village" (Breivik and Wedgeworth *Libraries* 14). These elements must be present if a climate of excellence is to be maintained. Probably the most important task for the librarian is to help empower the student to learn. Every librarian is a teacher; the librarian's activities relate directly or indirectly to learning and to creating a climate where learning can take place. In 1931, Edith Coulter said that teaching students how to discover information for themselves, providing materials to permit faculty to keep up-to-date in their fields, and providing specialized information to the community were the three functions of the community college library (Dale 233). Teaching is still the most important function today, especially if teaching is understood in the broadest sense, not as an activity restricted to the classroom. John Dewey first proposed that the school library be placed in the center of the school, so that the role of books in the learning process could be dramatized (United States 22). Frank Newman puts it this way: "It takes skill to empower a student to become a learner, to excite the student about wanting to learn, to draw on sources of information, knowledge and ideas. That is exactly what a good librarian does . . . but the ideal librarian, as far as students go, is someone who does all those things and engages students in a learning process" (Breivik and Wedgeworth *Libraries* 180). The librarian's task is central: to serve as filter in selecting, acquiring, and organizing the best in information; to help students become information literate; to help them develop a passion for learning. As librarians, we must teach students not only how to answer questions, but also how to question answers.

If a climate of excellence is to flourish, every member of the professional and support staff must be empowered to succeed. Many of the concepts of excellence that Tom Peters writes of are applicable to librarianship. He speaks of MBWA, "Management By Walking Around." All of us manage at least someone or something in the library. Librarians must be knowledgeable of the dynamics as well as the details of the library. What we do is LBWA, "Librarianship By Walking Around." Ask the students how they're doing, or if they need help. What sources are they using? What books are on the tables and in the carrels? What journals are being read?

What books have pages torn out? What is happening in the
building? Peters speaks of the importance of listening; many
ideas come from support staff, from students, from faculty
and administrators (*Passion* 10). Are we listening? Are we
hearing and responding to their comments? What do our
students think they want? What do they really want?

Developing Community

A corollary to LBWA is LBGOB, "Librarianship By Getting Out of the Building." When librarians stay on their own
turf they are working only with the committed. Working with
faculty and administrators on committees, in the faculty senate, and in the union helps to develop collegiality and reinforces the concept of librarians as academic peers.

If librarians are to function as peers, they need the opportunity to expand their professional skills. Administrators must
provide opportunities for librarians to do graduate work, to
do research, to attend conferences, to apply for sabbaticals or
professional leaves. Providing free tuition will permit librarians to immerse themselves in the language of specific content
areas. Community college librarians must be generalists; such
educational opportunities will permit them to learn at least
the basic concepts of particular disciplines. The librarians'
workload must be adjusted to meet these academic needs.
Faculty development is no less important for librarians than
for teachers. These academic issues may also be addressed
through the collective bargaining process.

Librarians must participate in the intellectual life of the
campus. They must not only serve on committees; they must
chair them. Such participation adds to the credibility of librarians. These campus activities also provide forums where librarians can listen to faculty and thus better understand the
frustrations and challenges of classroom teaching. Because
librarians function across departmental and divisional lines,
they are less likely to be seen as campus threats. This connectivity should be exploited to develop a sense of community on
campus. Boyer says that we "must find ways to strengthen the
connections between the classroom and other learning resources on the campus" (Breivik and Gee *Information* 7).

Schmoozing, informal conversations within the library and among other campus constituencies, enables librarians to communicate informally with their constituencies: they can mention new titles that have been received; they can let faculty know which assignments are giving students trouble; they can ask faculty for help in evaluating the collection in their areas of expertise; they can suggest challenging research assignments. Informal dialogues are not meant to replace more formal communication through annual reports, bibliographies, and library newsletters; they complement them.

"Soft reporting" is particularly helpful in getting out the library's message—those anecdotes, announcements, brief notes to the president and administrators that are so important. If all your microfilm machines are out of order on the same day, tell the president. If all the seats are filled in the reference area, tell the president. When the library has a landmark statistic, tell the president. Librarians must become proactive, not merely reactive, and reporting these and other incidents that highlight the drama of library life also serves to demonstrate excellence. Asp agrees that telling the library story in human terms is essential: "Snowing legislators with statistics and data isn't going to have the effect that giving them three or four stories of folks who have benefited from the service will" (Riggs 41).

Ownership

Positive library experiences help create a climate that contributes to what Peters calls ownership. Those who believe they own their jobs perform better, and leaders are those who believe everyone can learn to own his or her job. Ownership is essential if a climate of excellence is to be created. As librarians, we must be leaders as well as teachers. We must create a climate which permits both the information consumer and the worker to excel. Peters says there is no magic, "only people who find and nurture champions, dramatize company goals and direction, build skills and teams, spread irresistible enthusiasm. They are cheerleaders, coaches, storytellers and wanderers. They encourage, excite, listen, facilitate . . . You know they take their priorities seriously because they live them clearly and visibly; they walk the talk" (*Passion* 324).

Librarians would agree that constant attention must be given to the people who use our libraries, the students, our "customers." Yet if a climate of excellence is to be created, developing ownership-trust is important for all who work in the library. It is particularly important, however, for the support staff who are generally overworked and underpaid. One small way to encourage excellence is by giving symbolic rewards, since promotions are so difficult to achieve. The rewards may be as simple as a thank-you note, an occasional party, or a symbolic reward. Farewell parties, for example, are routine; one of our most successful symbolic occasions was a survival party—for those who *stayed*. On another occasion, everyone who worked in our library received a personal note with a gold star for excellence: one was cited for excellence in shelf reading; another for helping students with the *Readers' Guide;* a third for skill in acquisitions. Most kept those gold stars on their desks for months! Taking symbolic action is essential if a positive institutional climate is to be developed (Kouzes 247).

The search for excellence in the library takes time, but eventually people respond to attention and to high expectations. As Peters says, "We are emotional creatures. We feel pride, we feel slights. Our life is a drama to each of us. The winners are institutions and leaders that own up to that reality and live with us as humans—not as automatons" (*Passion* 277). Once the climate becomes positive, where individuals are allowed to own their jobs, to experiment, even to fail on occasion, then their work will improve, and the perception of the library will also become more positive. Hans Selye, an expert on stress said, "If you do what you like, you never really work. Your work is your play" (Siegel 168).

Relating Management Literature to Library Literature

Library literature, too, is beginning to address the issue of excellence. Georgi and Bellanti speak of interdependent variables, strategy skills, staff, style, systems, shared values, and structure (3). Judy Labovitz cites Peters; she too emphasizes the importance of support staff, recommends cross-training, paying attention, stroking, communication, and discussion (Georgi 7). Staff development programs are means of achieving excellence. At our library, for the past ten years, one day each semester has been set aside for staff development. Librarians and support staff meet to discuss a range of issues. Guest speakers from various departments on campus are brought in to discuss their work and its impact on the library. Everyone's opinion is sought, and people listen and learn to communicate. Communication is critical if cooperation and excellence are to be achieved.

Perception and symbolism also play a part even here. For example, is the door to your director's office open most of the time, or is he or she shut off from the department? Are reference desks set in highly visible areas so that students perceive the librarians are there to help them, or must students search for librarians as well as information? Are librarians "stapled" to those desks, or do they walk over with students to help them learn how to use a particular source? Does a small fortress of "ready reference" books separate the students from the personal interaction they need so badly if they are to succeed in the search for information literacy?

Meryl Swanigan speaks of the "skunk works" Peters emphasized, where small groups of workers go off to talk, research, collaborate on projects (Georgi 15). People are encouraged to experiment to improve services. Success with skunk works is not critical; the process is. Dumont and Dougherty both speak of the need to develop trust, to encourage risk taking, even if there is a chance of failure (Riggs 109, 146). Asp, in discussing a decision to initiate statewide reciprocal borrowing, admitted that many were fearful of the outcome. "It was taking the plunge, it was being brave enough to make the decision to try it, to test it; that was the crucial thing" (Riggs 143). This is somewhat analogous to what we want our students to do—to experiment with information in order to develop competence and success.

Libraries often equate excellence with what is measurable: numbers of titles and volumes, numbers of items circulated, numbers of reference questions answered. The temptation is to measure what is quantifiable rather than what may really be essential to good library service. Young suggests that behavior may be an important measure in reference service. An appropriate goal, for example, might be that the reference librarian relate positively to the user. Some behaviors that could indicate the achievement of the goal would include: "appears approachable to patrons by smiling, maintaining eye contact, being attentive, and listening carefully" ("Methods" 73). James Matarazzo says that the staff practicing excellence knows its industry: "they are excited about oil or eyewash" (592). Vaselakis puts it this way: "And nothing must ever be too much trouble to do. Nothing. Ever. I don't want to hear someone say, well I can't do that because I have to do this. Our customers don't want to hear that" (Riggs 104). In other words, passionate librarianship should not be an oxymoron but an expectation.

Mignon Adams speaks of the need to develop leadership behavior among our librarians. In order for leadership to flourish, she stresses being involved in committee work, understanding the college mission, and serving in community positions. Management may also foster excellence by rotating job assignments and encouraging continuing education and professional development. She also emphasizes that library directors shouldn't overreact to mistakes. "Mistakes . . . are an important ingredient of the learning process" (574). Flexibility and experimentation are necessary. A positive working climate may help to avoid the "intellectual arteriosclerosis" Rothstein speaks of. He describes three Canadian colleges: 35 of 50 librarians had been working in the same library for 12 to 22 years—if not in the same job, in the same area (34). Such job stagnation is most likely to result in library stagnation.

Perception

Perception is a real factor in the achievement of excellence. Evan Farber suggests we make sure the library is being run well before we embark on bibliographic instruction efforts. "Establish your reputation for doing what you're traditionally expected to do, then build on that" (Oberman-Soroka 399). Oberg et al. in their report on faculty perceptions of librarians indicate a clouded view of our work. They report that at Albion College, 77% of the respondents to their survey could not identify by name all five librarians, and 40% identified librarians as members of the support staff. The more the faculty had direct contact with the library, the higher they ranked the librarians (217, 225). Drake quotes John Guasperi, "In the final analysis, perceived quality is the only quality that matters since what the customer perceives is what the customer receives" (527).

Ownership, trust, communication, experimentation, positive perceptions combine to create empowerment and excellence. The library that has created a climate of excellence is then in a position to help empower the students to develop the skills and strategies needed for lifelong learning.

The Library Culture

The library culture is meant to develop the passion for learning, not to create a scene of quiet misunderstanding, where students silently struggle, wander aimlessly as they search the collection, only to fail in their research. In a library of excellence, the students are paramount and resources serve to help them succeed in their drive for information literacy. Once the climate of excellence has evolved, academic synergy can take place. When academic synergy occurs, all those in the library, especially the students, know they are part of a learning environment. When the librarians and staff feel that they learn something new each day, that sense will be communicated to the students. When the students feel accepted with their academic strengths and weaknesses, they will be free to experiment with information and will then develop skills they might not have thought within their capability. It is this sense of community, the creation of academic linkages, which will create a learning climate.

Think of the students in the library at any given time. While many are engaged in traditional library activities—research, reading, studying—others are there for reasons that might not seem academic in nature. They're talking, sleeping, socializing, or just sitting. Why? If the climate of the library is positive, they may be there because they want to "feel" academic. They're joining together in a learning community, learning that it's acceptable to learn. They are surrounded by books and resources of all types, but they may also be reacting to a climate that is new to them and that the librarians must exploit in a positive way. Unlike dormitory schools, community colleges attract large numbers of part-time students, and commuter students with family and job responsibilities who often find studying at home difficult at best.

LBWA, "Librarianship By Walking Around," is one way we can help students to develop academic self-esteem, and reinforce the concept of a library culture at the same time. Ask students how they are; encourage group study—in an appropriate place in the building. If they seem upset or puzzled, offer to help. Encourage recreational reading. Often that connection can save a marginal student. Follow up with a call to a professor if necessary. Two of our librarians became so student oriented that they started new clubs, one for international students and one for Far Eastern students. International Night is now one of the most successful student events on campus.

Many community college librarians know that their students return to the community college library even after they transfer, because they feel better there. Perhaps it's that they are comfortable with the familiar. If, however, they learned to learn there, if they learned to connect with a particular librarian, if they learned that it is not only appropriate to ask questions but necessary to do so if they expect to succeed, if they have learned that learning is difficult and often frustrating, if they have learned to persist in spite of those difficulties, then the library culture has had a positive effect. Students at community colleges are impatient, often because they are working long hours in addition to attending school. They are "frustrated to learn that the library reference desk is not a McDonald's service counter where quick stops yield fast information in neat take-out containers" (Breivik and Wedgeworth *Libraries* 46).

Webster's defines *culture* as "development, improvement, or refinement of the mind, emotions, interests, manners, taste, etc." There is a library culture; how positive it is depends in part on how much of a climate of excellence has been created. Boyer speaks of the "culture of information" (Breivik and

Wedgeworth *Libraries* 22), and says it is the library's responsibility to promote it. How can this occur when, on average, 25% of undergraduates spend no time in the library during a normal week, and 65% use it four or fewer hours per week? (Breivik and Gee *Information* 42). One way to increase successful use of the library is to think of it not merely as the research center of the campus, but as its academic culture center as well. In order to do this, it is necessary to look carefully at who uses the library and what happens there.

Demographics and Cultural Diversity: A Challenge

First of all, more and more students are attending community colleges. A random survey of 50 community colleges indicates fall 1989 enrollment was up 5.7%: up 7% in Virginia, 9% in Minnesota, 4% in Maryland (Reinhard "Enrollment Up" 1). More and more community college students are women: 264,000 more in 1989 than in 1985 (Reinhard "Enrollment Up" 1). At CUNY (City University of New York), 64% of the student enrollment is female (Breivik and Wedgeworth *Libraries* 44). California expects its population to hit 40 million in this decade, resulting in an increase of 400,000 students; plans are underway for 16 new community colleges there (Ramsy 1).

The profile of our students is changing. In 1890 more than 50% of the American people worked on the farm or in occupations related to the farm. Today only 2% of the working population is involved in such occupations (Parnell 103). Dramatic demographic changes have already had and will continue to have an impact on our libraries. The mean earnings of men in the twenty- to twenty-four-year-old age group declined 41.6% between 1973 and 1984. Twenty-three percent of children under the age of three are in homes below the poverty level (Parnell 107). Nearly one-half of all Hispanics and more than one-third of all Blacks are under 18 years of age. Slightly more than one-quarter of White Americans are under 18. Community colleges enroll 55% of all Hispanic undergraduates, 57% of Native American college students, 42% of all Asian college-level students and 43% of Black college students (Commission 9). By the year 2000 immigrants, women, and minorities will constitute 80% of the new entrants in the work force (Kappner 17).

Clearly these shifts in population must be addressed by librarians as they consider how to meet the educational needs of their user populations. The needs of the international students must be considered. Librarians must become knowledgeable about issues affecting minorities and ethnics. What are their learning patterns? Some first-generation college students may not be coming from an environment that values education: how can the library help to create a positive learning environment? How can librarians avoid the trap of stereotyping cultures they know little or nothing about? How can the careful selection and purchase of ethnically oriented resources help develop student self-esteem, and create a learning culture as well? What techniques can librarians learn which will set up an environment of trust, where the students feel accepted even if their grammar is poor or if they have accents? As Kflu and Loomba point out, if you dislike the professor, you hate the course; if you dislike the librarian, you can come to hate the library (6).

Not only are our community college students coming from increasingly diverse ethnic and cultural backgrounds, they are graying as well. In 1960, 90% of all men between fifty-five and sixty-five were in the work force; today only 75% of that age group are still working (Parnell *Dateline* 199). Many of those older workers are returning to school. With the advent of older students, the educational climate changes. Today it is estimated that 15% of the community college enrollment already hold college degrees (Parnell *Dateline* 199). Add to this academic mix a student whose learning history has been a negative one, and we have not only a rainbow of color, but a rainbow of educational experiences as well.

New Gateways to Excellence

Two relatively recent trends are likely to have a profound impact on the community college library. The first is the library's role in the development of information literacy, and the other, the library's role in economic development.

The American Library Association Presidential Committee

on Information Literacy issued a report on the topic in 1989. They describe an information-literate individual as one who is able to recognize when information is needed and, once the need is recognized, is then able to locate, evaluate, and effectively use that information (Ford 892). Rader points out that the issue is not bibliographic instruction versus information literacy, but the recognition of a responsibility to train individuals to cope in a technological world (20). Patricia Glass Schuman says that print illiteracy is now almost a national disease, with 23 million Americans unable to read above a fifth-grade level, and 20% of all Americans unable to write a legible check. "An individual must not only be print literate, he or she must be culturally literate, visually literate, and computer literate. With all these skills, the individual might then have a chance at being information literate" (35).

Librarians must accept their responsibility for the development of information literacy on their campus. Librarians teach skills the students are not likely to learn from classroom faculty. The librarian must recognize that, when working with the individual student, he or she is functioning as a teacher. Therefore, another task for the librarian is to become knowledgeable about appropriate learning strategies. The formal bibliographic instruction program is one step in the process but, as most librarians know, the process should be complemented and supplemented by the one-on-one interaction that may precede and/or follow the library instruction class.

Most of us have had the experience of students' returning to us days or weeks after we have connected with them, and finding that they expect us to remember either the specific reference questions asked or the topics of the papers! We also find that once the student has made the "librarian connection," then that librarian becomes the student's personal librarian and is consistently sought out every time help is needed. These occurrences point out the affective as well as the cognitive learning that takes place as a result of the librarian-student connection, the connection that is so vital if the student is to experience information success. "The more effective library will be the one actively reaching outward, formulating linkages to help clients broaden and refine their base of knowledge with resources from many places, and assuming fully the responsibility for having the trained staff and learning resources appropriate to its mission; for a chain of linkage is only as strong as the sum of the strength of each link" (United States 37).

The need for information literacy is not limited to students. Library automation is a reality: 40% of 1,050 colleges surveyed in 1989 had on-line library catalogs (Turner). The technology can become a tool for faculty development. Librarians know that faculty often can't or won't admit how little they know about library resources and library research. One study indicated that only 38% of scholars reported using on-line data bases, primarily because they didn't have the skills necessary to use the data bases (Breivik and Gee *Information* 58). Librarians can in a non-threatening way use automation as the catalyst for developing faculty information literacy.

Developing an information-literate faculty should enhance the information-literacy process for students, because if faculty do not see the value of the learning activity, the students are certainly not likely to. The classroom instructor and the librarian together, creating academic synergy, can help the student to become an independent library user. Donald Ray states, "The teacher—knowing why you would want to discover something but not always how—commends to the library a class of students, who learn how to find a few things without knowing why" (148). However, the librarian and the teacher together can develop meaningful learning activities, experiences that are active, individualized, up-to-date, realistic, and challenging. The information-literate faculty member creates the climate for an information-literate student, and together with the librarian develop appropriate learning experiences. "A good learning experience imitates reality. Once students graduate no one is going to stop work to lecture them each time they need to learn something new for their job. No one is going to hand them a textbook or reading list. No one is going to put books on reserve for them" (Breivik and Wedgeworth *Libraries* 34).

What also must be stressed if successful strategies are to be implemented is that students can learn. The climate of excellence requires that all who work in the library have high expectations for the students. A negative self-fulfilling prophecy is unacceptable. Dale Parnell puts it this way, "The major finding from educational research in the last thirty years is that the most important difference among learners is speed. There are fast learners and there are slow learners, there are no dumb students and there are no smart students" (*Dateline* 16). Information literacy is an economic as well as a lifelong learning issue. Information-literate individuals should be able to transfer those skills to their jobs and utilize them throughout their lives. Transferability is a requisite for success. "If college graduates working in the credit department of a bank do not know to consult library resources when seeking information related to a loan recommendation, those people are information illiterate whether or not they hold a Phi Beta Kappa key" (Breivik and Wedgeworth *Libraries* 37). While librarians may be alert to the need to develop information literacy for their students, they may need to learn why and how the library plays a role in economic development, a role which may add to the success of the college and community and of the library itself.

The second gateway is the library's role in economic development. Local governmental agencies and corporations are turning to colleges for assistance. They may need economic surveys, training, facilities, equipment, and professional staff. Parnell says that community colleges are becoming the convenience stores for small business assistance (*Dateline* 54). There are more than 11 million owners of small businesses in this country (Parnell *Dateline* 63). Sonia Nazario reporting in the *Wall Street Journal* indicates that more than 40,000 aviation mechanics will be needed in the next ten years, that more than 75% of job classifications will require post-secondary training for entry-level positions, and that perpetual retraining will soon become a reality. Small- and medium-sized companies provide 70% of the nation's jobs (22–23). What does this mean to the community college library?

Librarians must look at their role as information experts in a world flooded with data. More than one million books are published annually. There are now five times more words in the English language than there were in Shakespeare's day. The quantity of printed information is doubling every five years (Schuman 34). Librarians are the experts at organizing information; they are people oriented; they can retrieve information effectively; they network. These skills must be used by the college in order to help the college and the community meet its information needs. If in real estate the three most important criteria are location, location, location, then the three most important criteria to the librarian in terms of the library's role in economic development may be access, access, access. Yet, it cannot be "access to excess," as Schuman points out (33).

What are the major industries in the community? What sort of information do they need? Contacts with local businesses may lead to meaningful research assignments, real-life assignments for the students. Many community college libraries offer full borrowing privileges to county residents and employees. On a larger scale, in response to community needs, CARL (the Colorado Alliance of Research Libraries) created a system to link local business directly to the library. More than 25,000 people use it on a daily basis, producing 1.6 million transactions. "What businesses can gain from relationships with academic libraries is physical access to research collections and intellectual access to people with expertise in the structure of information sources" (Breivik and Wedgeworth *Libraries* 135).

In New York, Dr. Joseph Hankin, President of Westchester Community College, worked with county officials to permit a consortium of academic, public, and school libraries to automate. By 1992, there were 49 member libraries in the consortium and a data base of more than 4.5 million records. In addition to the on-line public-access catalog (OPAC), members can access a Local News Index, the Government Printing Office Manual, ERIC, Peterson's College Guides, the Library of Congress Subject Headings, a local Union List of Serials, ABI/Inform, Periodical Abstracts, and Newspaper Abstracts from University Microfilms International. Medline, from the National Library of Medicine, will soon be available. Creative consortium pricing enables the participating libraries to lease data bases they could not have afforded individually.

Anne Woodsworth and others writing of the future research library address the conflict inherent in information delivery. With the marketing of information as a potential source of revenue, the philosophy of free access to all library services may be at risk (136). That conflict will not be resolved easily. But what can be done now is for community college librarians to examine the issue in terms of their responsibility to the college mission. What services must remain totally free? Is it now part of the mission of the library to deliver better information services to the business community? If so, what are the costs? How can those costs be defrayed, either through charge for service or by the college's allocating additional staff and personnel to perform the functions? If librarians do not begin to address the issue, it may be decided for them by others as the college seeks to respond to its economic role in the community. How can the library sell its expertise to the college administration? If research is a major responsibility of the college, and the college can get funding from the business community in exchange for its research, how can the library become an active agent in the process? At the very least, providing open access to local business would be an inexpensive symbolic gesture. Librarians must become part of the information loop on campus. How many librarians work with the computer experts on their campus or with the computer experts of their sponsor? Might not such cooperative ventures improve services for all constituencies on campus in need of information and information delivery?

Challenges

Dale Parnell says that a key to institutional climate development in the 1990s will be institutional and staff renewal. "It is an important leadership task to encourage creativity, diversity, and even dissent—without tearing up the college" (*Dateline* 27). The same applies to the library.

Yet, possibly the most discouraging element in our work as librarians is the realization that, for whatever reasons, many of our faculty and administrators are not aware of what we are doing, what we have accomplished, what we hope to accomplish. William Moffett put it most effectively: "For all our meetings, conferences, and preconferences, for all our committees and task forces, our journals and yearbooks, are we any better understood by the clients in whose behalf we labor? By the senior officials who control our budgets and make information policy for our institutions? We talk too much to each other and not enough to them" (609).

Our need to talk to professionals other than librarians is absolutely essential. We must write in non-library journals and attend conferences of college educators, not just librarians. We must reach out to other audiences. We must read articles on higher education in general and community colleges in particular. We must seek out public and school librarians. For example, in an attempt to improve articulation, the Library Association of the City University of New York co-sponsored with the Library Unit of the New York City Board of Education an institute, "Instructional Perspectives: A Dialogue Between High School and College Librarians."

In a *Nation at Risk,* a report prepared by the National Commission on Excellence in Education, the roles of librarians and libraries were not mentioned as essential elements in the search for educational excellence. In *Building Communities,* published by the Commission on the Future of Community Colleges, American Association of Community and Junior Colleges, libraries are juxtaposed with the cafeteria and the business office (30). We must pay attention to this communication chasm. There is excellence in our libraries; there is community in our libraries; there is learning taking place in our libraries. Why is it that those in the library know this, but the policymakers do not?

Because of the heavy demands of community college students, their need for intensive one-on-one assistance, their often poor academic and library experiences, we are all overworked. However, we must set new priorities, for unless we learn to communicate accurately, consistently, and meaningfully to those who control our academic destiny, our libraries will continue to be viewed as the heart of the college, but a heart with valves that are clogged.

Community college libraries, their role, their often unique functions in terms of resources and academic support, are barely mentioned in our library schools, so obviously there is a learning gap there, too. Those of us who have made a commitment to our community college libraries care deeply about them. We know that what we do, we do well. As Schuman says, "No technology can beat the highly developed skill of a librarian who can analyze an information problem, figure out the real underlying questions, and match those questions with answers. No machine can compete with a creative, knowledgeable, flexible, professional librarian, one who provides interpersonal interaction, information evaluation, communication, synthesis, and judgment" (38). We know we are accomplishing much, yet much of what we achieve is unmeasurable. We must find better ways to communicate about our library community, about the special things we do, about how we represent the college and the community in microcosm. We must also learn how to assess what we do. These are some of our tasks for the next decade if we are to have the opportunity to continue to do what we do best: to empower our students to learn, to grow, to succeed. Mae West said, "Too much of a good thing is simply wonderful" (Parnell *Dateline* 27). Community college libraries are simply wonderful; they are centers of learning, and within them librarians build myriad moments of excellence.

The following chapters will reflect moments of excellence: excellence in the urban, rural, technical and Canadian community colleges, excellence in the classroom, excellence in the librarian/teacher connection, excellence in learning resource centers, and excellence in managing as well as in planning for the future. The community college library, whether it be called a library, a learning resource center, or a learning resources center, should literally and symbolically be the center of excellence on the campus.

Works Cited

"Academia's Other Half." *U.S. News and World Report* 16 Oct. 1989: 82–83.

Adams, Mignon. "The Role of Academic Libraries in Teaching and Learning." *College and Research Libraries News* July–Aug. 1992: 442–45.

Adams, Mignon, et al. "Developing College Library Leaders of Tomorrow." *College and Research Libraries News* July 1989: 573–74.

AECT-ACRL Joint Committee. "Standards for Two-Year College Learning Resources Programs: A Draft." *College and Research Libraries News* June 1989: 496–505.

Affleck, Mary Ann. "Bibliographic Instruction in Community Colleges: Current Practice and the New Standards." *Research Strategies* Winter 1992: 24–33.

Alexander, Suzanne. "Research Firm Taps Oceans of Data to Bail Out Clients." *Wall Street Journal* 3 Apr. 1990, eastern ed., sec. B: 2.

American Library Association Presidential Committee on Information Literacy. Chicago: ALA, 1989.

Armes, Nancy, and Kay McClenney. "Mirror Mirror: Challenges for Colleges in Building Communities." *AACJC Journal* Apr.–May 1989: 17–21.

Asheim, Lester. "Ortega Revisited." *Library Quarterly* July 1982: 215–26.

Bell, Terrel. "The Dropout Problem: Untouched by the Education Reform Movement." Editorial. *Community, Technical, and Junior College Times* 1 Aug. 1989: 2.

Bierbaum, Esther Green. "The Two-Year College LRC: Promise Deferred?" *College and Research Libraries* Nov. 1990: 531–38.

Bock, Joleen D. "From Libraries to Learning Resources: Six Decades of Progress—And Still Changing." *Community and Junior College Libraries* Winter 1984:35–45.

Breivik, Patricia Senn, "Making the Most of Libraries." *Change* July 1987: 44–52.

Breivik, Patricia Senn, and E. Gordon Gee. *Information Literacy: Revolution in the Library.* New York: Macmillan, 1989.

Breivik, Patricia Senn, and Ward Shaw. "Libraries Prepare for an Information Age." *Educational Record* Winter 1989: 13–19.

Breivik, Patricia Senn, and Robert Wedgeworth, eds. *Libraries and the Search for Academic Excellence.* Metuchen, N.J.: Scarecrow, 1988.

Commission on the Future of Community Colleges. *Building Communities.* Washington, D.C.: AACJC, 1988.

"Community College Learning Resources Achievement Awards." *Community and Junior College Libraries* 6.2 (1989): 89–91.

Currie, William W. "Evaluating the Collection of a Two-Year Branch Campus by Using Textbook Citations." *Community and Junior College Libraries* 6.2 (1989): 73–79.

Dale, Doris Cruger. "The Learning Resource Center's Role in the Community College System." *College and Research Libraries* May 1988: 232–38.

Davis, Erik. "Cyberlibraries." *Lingua Franca* Feb–Mar. 1992: 46–51.

De Angelis, Patrick. "Pedro's Question: Learning Resource Centers and the Community." *Library Journal* July 1987: 41–43.

DeLoughry, Thomas J. "Professors Are Urged to Devise Strategies to Help Students Deal with 'Information Explosion' Spurred by Technology." *Chronicle of Higher Education* 8 Mar. 1989: A13–A15.

Dervarics, Charles. "Report Documents Minority Dropout Rate in CC Vocational Programs." *Community College Week* 2 Oct. 1989: 7.

Dougherty, Richard M. "Research Library Networks: Leveraging the Benefits." *Academe* July–Aug. 1989: 22–25.

Drake, Miriam A. "Management of Information." *College and Research Libraries* Sep. 1989: 521–31.

Eels, Walter Crosby. "Junior College Libraries." *Junior College Journal* Jan. 1936: 202–6.

"Enrollment Up at Community Colleges in Colorado." *Community College Week* 2 Oct. 1989.

Farris, Deirdre A. "Library Automation at a Multi Campus Community College." *Library Software Review* May–June 1987: 123–27.

Ford, Barbara J. "Information Literacy." Editorial. *College & Research Libraries* July 1991: 313–14.

———. "Information Literacy." *College and Research Libraries News* Nov. 1989: 892–93.

Georgi, Charlotte, and Robert Bellanti, eds. *Excellence in Library Management.* New York: Haworth Press, 1985.

Hisle, Lee W. "Learning Resource Services in the Community College: On the Road to the Emerald City." *College and Research Libraries* Nov. 1989: 613–25.

Holleman, Margaret, ed. *The Role of the Learning Resources Center in Instruction.* New Directions for Community Colleges 71. San Francisco: Jossey-Bass, 1990.

Kflu, Tesfai, and Mary Loomba. "Academic Libraries and the Culturally Diverse Student Population." *College and Research Libraries News* June 1990: 524–27.

Kniffel, Leonard. "A Standing Ovation for the Omission of Libraries." Editorial. *American Libraries* Sep. 1991.

Kouzes, James M., and Barry Z. Posner. *The Leadership Challenge.* San Francisco: Jossey-Bass Publishers, 1988.

Leatherman, Courtney. "Two of Six Regional Accrediting Agencies Take Steps to Prod Colleges on Racial, Ethnic Diversity." *Chronicle of Higher Education* 15 Aug. 1990: 1 + .

Lewis, Peter H. "Where the Libraries Are Leading the Way." *New York Times* 13 May 1990, city ed., sec. 3: 8.

Lutzker, Marilyn. "Bibliographic Instruction and Accreditation in Higher Education." *College and Research Libraries News* Jan. 1990: 14–18.

MacAdam, Barbara. "Information Literacy: Models for the Curriculum." *College and Research Libraries News* Nov. 1990: 948–51.

Martin, Susan K. "Information Technology and Libraries: Toward the Year 2000." *College and Research Libraries* July 1989: 397–405.

Matarazzo, James M. "A Field Study Defines Corporate Library Excellence." *American Libraries* Sep. 1986: 588–92.

Miller, Tim. "Data Bases: Finding Your World in the Electronic Newspaper." *Editor and Publisher* 10 Sep. 1988: 34–44.

Moffett, William A. "Talking to Ourselves." Editorial. *College and Research Libraries* Nov. 1989: 609–10.

Molholt, Pat. "Libraries and the New Technologies: Courting the Cheshire Cat." *Library Journal* 15 Nov. 1988: 37–41.

Mosley, Madison M., Jr. "Mission Statements for the Community College LRC." *College and Research Libraries News* Nov. 1988: 653–54.

Nazario, Sonia L. "Bearing the Brunt: Community Colleges Must Train Many of the Nation's Workers, But They May Not Be Up to the Job." *Wall Street Journal* 9 Feb. 1990, eastern ed., sec. R: 22–23.

Newman, Frank. "Adapting Academic Libraries to the Future." Editorial. *Change* July 1987: 4–5.

O'Banion, Terry. "The Golden Age of Community Colleges." Editorial. *Community College Week* 16 Apr. 1990: 5.

Oberg, Larry R., Mary Kay Schleiter, and Michael Van Houten. "Faculty Perceptions of Librarians at Albion College: Status, Role, Contribution, and Contacts." *College and Research Libraries* Mar. 1989: 215–30.

Oberman-Soroka, Cerise, ed. *Proceedings from the Southeastern Conference on Approaches to Bibliographic Instruction, March 16–17, 1978.* Charleston, S.C.: College of Charleston, 1978.

Parnell, Dale. *Dateline 2000.* Washington, D.C.: The Community College Press, 1990.

———. "Enrollment: The Untold Story." Editorial. *Community, Technical, and Junior College Times* 24 Apr. 1990: 1.

Peters, Thomas, and Robert H. Wateman, Jr. *In Search of Excellence: Lessons Learned from America's Best-Run Companies.* New York: Harper and Row, 1982.

Peters, Thomas J., and Nancy Austin. *A Passion for Excellence: The Leadership Difference.* New York: Random House, 1985.

Rader, Hannelore. "Bibliographic Instruction or Information Literacy." *College and Research Libraries News* Jan. 1990: 18–20.

Ramsy, M. A. "Sixteen More Colleges Proposed for California." *Community College Week* 2 Oct. 1989: 1.

Ray, Donald. "The Meaningful and the Procedural: Dilemmas of the Community College Library." *Journal of Academic Librarianship* 15.3 (1989): 147–50.

Reinhard, Bill. "Enrollment Continues to Grow Steadily at Nation's Community, Technical Colleges." *Community, Technical, and Junior College Times* 12 Sep. 1989.

———. "Enrollment Up Dramatically, AACJC Survey Finds." *Community, Technical, and Junior College Times* 24 Oct. 1989: 1+.

Ridgeway, Trish. "Information Literacy: An Introductory Reading List." *College and Research Libraries News* July 1990: 645–48.

Riggs, Donald E., and Gordon A. Sabine. *Libraries in the '90s. What the Leaders Expect.* New York: Oryx Press, 1988.

Rose, Mike. *Lives on the Boundary: The Struggles and Achievements of America's Underprepared.* New York: Free-Macmillan, 1989.

Rothstein, Samuel. "Professional Staff in Canadian University Libraries." *Library Journal* Nov. 1986: 31–34.

Rouche, John. "Excellence and the Community College Mission." Editorial. *Community, Technical, and Junior College Times* 12 Sep. 1989: B3.

Schuman, Patricia Glass. "Reclaiming Our Technological Future." *Library Journal* 1 Mar. 1990: 34–38.

Segal, John. "Library Networking in 1988." *The Bowker Annual of Library and Book Trade Information.* New York: Bowker, 1989.

Sheridan, Jean. "WAC and Libraries: A Look at the Literature." *Journal of Academic Librarianship* May 1992: 90–94.

Siegel, Bernie S. *Love, Medicine and Miracles.* New York: Harper, 1986.

Smith, Al, and Darline Morris. "Presidential Perspectives on Teaching and Learning." *AACJC Journal* Apr.–May 1989: 30–36.

Smith, D. J. "An Examination of Higher Education: A View from the College Library." *Journal of Academic Librarianship* 15.3 (1989): 140–46.

Spannbauer, Paul M. "The HVCC Database Research Project: Information On-Line/On-Disc." *Colleague* (1990): 51–56.

"Standards for Community, Junior and Technical College Learning Resources Programs." *College and Research Libraries News* Sep. 1990: 757–67.

Turner, Judith Axler. "Computer Notes." *Chronicle of Higher Education* 20 Sep. 1989: A17.

United States. Department of Education. Office of Educational Research and Improvement. Center for Libraries and Education Improvement. *Alliance for Excellence: Librarians Respond to A NATION AT RISK.* Washington: GPO, 1984.

Watters, Robert D. "A Climate of Excellence: Paving the Way for Student Success at Miami-Dade South's Library." *Community and Junior College Libraries* 4.4 (1986): 7–27.

Webster's New World Dictionary, second college ed., 1970, s.v. "culture."

Weiskel, Timothy. "The Electronic Library and the Challenge of Information Planning." *Academe* July–Aug. 1989: 8–12.

White, Herbert S. "Bibliographic Instruction, Information Literacy, and Information Empowerment." *Library Journal* Jan. 1992: 76–78.

Wiley, Ed III. "Community College Leaders Say Increasing Priority." *Community College Week* 16 Oct. 1989: 14.

———. "Prison Education Attempts to Restore Hope." *Community College Week* 2 Oct. 1989: 1+.

Woodsworth, Anne, et al. "The Model Research Library: Planning for the Future." *Journal of Academic Librarianship* 15.3 (1989): 132–38.

Young, William F. "Methods for Evaluating Reference Desk Performance." *RQ* Fall 1985: 69–75.

THE EFFECTIVE LEARNING RESOURCES CENTER MANAGER FOR THE 1990'S

Antoinette M. Kania

The world into which community colleges have matured is technologically complex, politically sophisticated, economically depressed, and socially and culturally diverse. The impact of this world on the community college as an institution and on those within it who are charged with the responsibility for its management is enormous. With their own concomitant "increasing complexities, college libraries of the future will require highly trained and effective leaders" (Adams p. 574) to respond to the demands created by this "nineties" environment. Most of these requirements for effective management go much beyond the scope of the library manager's own discipline and usually much beyond his/her own formal training. More and more community college learning resources center administrators will be as much "chosen for their demonstrated managerial competence and leadership" (Moran p. 31) as for their professional knowledge for developing and providing LRC services to students and faculty.

The LRC director who will be a leader must have "a wider view," which includes, in the broadest sense, not only knowledge about developments in the academic library world, but also knowledge about developments in higher education in general, particularly with a view to how those developments may affect the community college (Adams 1989). At the same time, the director must have a clear understanding of the mission of his/her own particular institution, and of the real and potential role the LRC will play in the educational process within the institution. The LRC must have the kind of leadership that can effectively compete for the LRC's appropriate share of decreasing institutional resources; that can motivate professional staff who are highly tenured, tired, and who tend not to have the broader view; and that can make library literate a student body that is ever more culturally diverse and educationally disadvantaged.

Accountability and Assessment

In striving to manage for excellence, the LRC director will operate neither alone nor in isolation of his/her institution or external environment. Today the public mandate in higher education, affecting virtually all institutions at the state and local level, is accountability and assessment (Ewell 1987; Finn 1988; Moore 1986; Spangehl 1987). Within this context, Patricia Breivik reminds us that such assessment requirements should "not go forward without examining the role of libraries" (Breivik p. 44). It will become increasingly important for learning resources centers to be able "to provide evidence that their programs and services are producing effective results, and that they are doing so with a level of demonstrated quality that consistently meets the needs of their users" (Kania 1990, p. 82). The LRC director will need to employ new methods and processes in order to be able to do so.

Similarly, K. Patricia Cross talks about two "wings" of this same assessment movement; one in which the politicians demand assessment of educational quality for public accountability purposes; and one in which educators and accreditors focus on assessment as a tool for improvement of performance at the institutional level (Cross p. 8). How the learning resources center, operating from its own place within the community college, can contribute to the improvement of performance of the institution in educating its students is at the heart of this chapter, and is ultimately the greatest challenge to the LRC manager in these times.

The learning resources center is accountable on several levels both internally and externally. It is first internally, and most immediately, accountable for the quality of its program to its students and faculty, then to its academic dean and president, and ultimately to its board of trustees. Externally, the LRC is accountable as a component part of its community college to its county sponsor, the state university system or district of which it may be a part, and last but not least, its

institution's accrediting agencies, both specialized and regional. The LRC is asked routinely by these constituencies to
present evidence of program quality in its annual reports,
budget proposals, grant applications, program reviews, and
self-studies in order to be funded, recognized, approved, or
accredited. Being able to do this well will require the use of
assessment models, which delineate the process and provide
the outcome data to substantiate achievement of program
goals and any claims to quality that the learning resources
center may need to justify.

It is assessment for improvement purposes which will enable the manager to 1) demonstrate the quality and viability of
the LRC program to get the institutional support and resources required to develop and grow, and 2) to identify those
areas in which improvements are indicated, to design inter-
ventions, and to conduct follow-up assessments to determine
if indeed improvement has occurred. It is a most credible
manager who can do this.

If the mandate is accountability, and the objective is improvement, then the "victory is in the process" (Kalick p. 28).
Even though it was fishing about which our editor, Rosanne
Kalick, was writing, her point is indeed very well taken and
equally applicable to management strategy, where the process
employed in the LRC to study, to plan, to evaluate, and to
recommend is the end as well as the means. Management is
working with and through others to achieve program goals.
How goals are accomplished can be as important as accomplishing the goals themselves, both from the point of view of
those *with* whom it is done and from the point of view of
those *for* whom it is done.

The three most important areas of management in which
the process will directly affect the results are self-study,
planning, and the management of change—all of which
should ultimately dovetail, and all of which will make use of
assessment models to direct the process. For the learning
resources center, then, self-study is to be understood as a
critical component of the planning cycle itself, where the
results of an activity or a service are analyzed in the light of
originally stated goals and objectives. Affecting and managing
change, too, is an outgrowth of both the self-study and the
planning process.

Self-Study

The model for academic library self-study has been described in detail by this author elsewhere (Kania 1990). It is based on the Kells self-study model for institutional and programmatic self-study (Kells 1988), but adapts the process for self-assessment to a learning resources center environment and includes both the use of academic library standards, the setting of measures of achievement in the local setting in relation to those standards, and the use of performance measures to assess the degree of achievement in determining the quality of the LRC's collections and services. Also included therein, as a practical guide to the process, is a start-to-finish hypothetical case study of one community college LRC's self-study process conducted for accreditation purposes. The intent of the original research on which this self-study work was based was 1) to provide the theoretical and practical rationale for conducting self-study in the academic library setting, and 2) to provide a much needed, useful, outcome-oriented guide to the self-study process itself (Kania 1988).

Briefly, the self-study case example in the above work employs the four phases of the Kells model—design, organization, execution, and implementation. The design of the study, or the plan of how to proceed, is the key to a successful self-study. Generally, for self-study purposes, the nature of the design is largely dependent on the amount of information available for purposes of analysis. The greater the need for data, the more comprehensive, or all inclusive, will be the design and, therefore, the study. The organization of the study includes the identification of committed and sympathetic leaders, the formulation of work groups that are natural groupings already (i.e., departments, councils, teams), particularly in small LRC settings, the sequencing of activities, and the development of time lines. The carrying out of the study itself in the execution phase includes the actual committee work—data gathering, discussion, analysis, drafting reports, and making recommendations.

The last phase incorporates the implementation of the results of the self-study, and the establishment of a follow-up group and process to monitor progress on implementation of the recommendations. Staff must have reasonable expectations that the results of their efforts will be implemented. The degree to which an LRC can "absorb the results of the process" (Williams p. 159) and in doing so, can establish the beginnings of a planning cycle, is the degree to which the evaluation process has been successful. As well, the level of success of the self-study will be determined by the occurrence of a wide range of staff participation and the extent to which there has been effective communication about the process within the learning resources center and, equally important, throughout the college.

Planning

However, self-study is not enough. Koenig and Kerson describe self-study as "positioning rather than planning" (p. 201). That is not to imply that self-study is not a worthwhile process, but just that it is only one piece of a larger process—planning. While self-study is useful, because its intention is to lead to corrective measures, or improvement, in and of itself, self-study is not "proactive planning for a future environment that may differ in very significant ways from the present" (p. 201).

As an unsuspecting diner recently, I was reminded of the value of planning from another perspective. Breaking open a fortune cookie at my favorite Chinese restaurant, I found the declaration that "good luck is the result of good planning." As with other management tools, there are "the believers and non-believers" (McClure p. 7), but my fortune served as a useful reminder that the "good luck" of others is most likely a result of effective planning.

The very simplest dictionary definition of *planning* suffices—"having a specific goal or purpose . . . [and] formulating a program for the accomplishment of [that] goal" (*American Heritage*). The definition sounds straightforward enough, however, it is in the doing of it that we are all tested. When effectively employed, planning can be that process which anticipates student and faculty needs, creates new initiatives, and prepares the learning resources center for change and for coping with the known and unknown future. Yet, Stueart and Moran tell us that it is "one of the most easily avoided activities in libraries" (p.19). Have we not all heard the complaints about "bad luck" or "circumstances beyond our control" that caused something to happen, when, in fact, what is more likely the case is the absence of a systematic planning effort to influence the outcome of events (Stueart and Moran 1987)?

Planning will give purpose and direction to the LRC effort. It will establish priorities to provide a basis for resource allocation and to assure that activities and services are focused and relevant; it will lead to improved services and operations by requiring the collecting and analysis of data and the setting of local standards of measure for assessing progress and/or achievement; it will motivate staff by uniting them in a common effort and in coordinated activities; and it will provide the LRC with a built-in public relations marketing tool, which will demonstrate to those to whom the LRC is accountable that it knows what it is that needs to be done, and that it can articulate what strategies it intends to employ in order to get there (McClure 1986; Stueart and Moran 1987).

Important to the effective implementation of the planning process is the environment in which planning takes place. As with the self-study effort, it must be wholly understood and supported by the LRC manager, who will set the tone for what will take place. Already overworked staff will need to know that their efforts in this time-consuming venture will not only be appreciated, but will result in real improvements and change. Everyone must have the opportunity to be involved, and staff training may need to take place. It must be a group effort, since the decisions made and the results of planning cannot be the work of one individual or one department. Planning should be ongoing, cyclical, and cybernetic; that is, plans should be updated and reviewed on a regular basis and be based on feedback from the process. Circumstances are likely to change and assumptions may need to be adjusted (Koenig and Kerson 1983).

The multi-dimensional Mackenzie model best represents and incorporates these concepts (1969). It was developed as a management tool not for libraries, of course, but for the corporate world, which, long before we did, understood the requirements of planning and accountability. The model is a useful one, not only because of its basic simplicity, but because of its recognition of the interrelationships inherent in all of its parts. In fact, it was Mackenzie's aim "not to give the executive new information, but to help him [or her] put the pieces together" (p. 80). Often referred to as "Mackenzie's wheel," the model is graphically displayed as concentric circles depicting three basic elements of the management or planning cycle.

First, Mackenzie suggests that at the heart of the process are three basic components—people, things, and ideas—which together provide the leadership, the administration, and the creativity to drive the process. Second, he identifies five functions that comprise the planning cycle itself, which are the sequential activities of the process: planning, organizing, staffing, directing, and controlling. Third are three functions which operate throughout the entire process: analyzing problems, making decisions, and communicating. Mackenzie calls these last three functions "general" or "continuous," since they will, or should, occur at every step along the way (p. 87). Problems that will need to be analyzed, and about which decisions will need to be made, will come to light in most every activity (if reality is truly to follow from theory), and effective communication strategies employed throughout the process will ensure its success. Mackenzie admits, as well, that as a matter of practicality, the various functions and activities may blend or merge with one another in the normal course of events. Not only is that normal, it may even be preferable.

It is not unusual that Mackenzie begins his management cycle with a planning activity. It is, in fact, the model's most important function, for it is here that the relationship between where one is and where one wishes to be is established. Similar to Kells' design phase for self-study, this planning stage will design the project and define its purpose. The focus will be on setting goals and objectives, against which measures of performance, or standards, are set, and for which the means of accomplishment are clearly, and specifically, outlined. It is here that alternatives are explored and priorities established.

In the organizing stage, the program is implemented. The organizational structure of the project is established with areas of responsibility carefully delineated. The roles and responsibilities are assigned to individuals and/or groups and the relationships between and among them are designated. When this particular piece is overlooked, things can so easily fall through the cracks and incidents of finger pointing can occur. Sound familiar?

The next stage is most likely to be implemented concurrently with organizing, because it involves not only the selecting but perhaps even the recruiting and training of staff. The staffing stage, in this author's mind, is probably that part of the process which is most neglected and/or undervalued, not only in our academic institutions at large, but in our learning resources centers as well. Individuals, professional and clerical alike, need to be oriented, fully briefed, and, if necessary, trained in order to understand and to be able to carry out a project and conduct its activities. We do this more successfully with the implementation of automation projects, probably because it is the most obvious. However, what about the less obvious ventures and programs that will often leave staff bewildered, recalcitrant, or just plain bored, such as faculty liaison services, collection evaluation, literacy programs, or integrated bibliographic instruction?

Another major stage in the planning process that also deals with the human factor is the directing stage, and one where leadership at middle management and supervisory levels will again be tested. Once organized, trained, and working, staff will need to be motivated, encouraged, rewarded, and indeed perhaps corrected along the way. The less the ambiguity about how it's going, about what the ongoing expectations for the project are, and about who the individuals are who are making it happen the better. Re-assignments may have to be made, slight alterations in the nature of an activity or task, and conflicts of all sorts—personal and professional—which are sure to arise, will need to be managed and resolved.

The controlling stage brings us full circle, back to what is both the end and the beginning of the process. It is that part of the planning process which incorporates its own requirements for self-study. The definition of *controlling* here is to be taken in the context of quality control, asking the questions, "Have we produced (created, conducted) the best product (service, program) of which we are capable? If not, why not? And how can it be done better the next time?" Using the principles of self-study in this last stage in the process, results are measured and analyzed against the original intentions (i.e., goals and objectives), and level of success is determined so that, if necessary, corrective action be taken, and the results improved in the next cycle.

Mackenzie's model emphasizes the "behavioristic," and that is why its importance should not be overlooked. As he himself says, "It elevates staffing and communicating to the level of a function" (p. 87), so that the individuals and how they interrelate are recognized as integral to the process. In this model, the understanding of the need to employ a planning, or management, process is equal with the understanding of the importance of the individuals who will be involved. These individuals will be involved intimately with another threesome—collaboration, consensus, and coalitions. All of these behaviors are integral to implementing change which, in effect, is the intended outcome of planning and self-study.

Management of Change

Done well, planning and self-study will lead to change. Using these processes and their people resources, learning resources centers can "develop the capacity to adapt themselves to changing situations should the need arise" (Williams p. 152), and, in fact, determine the very nature and direction of the change itself. Planned change is improvement oriented, and it incorporates the use of these evaluation and management processes as an adaptive device on one hand and as a purposeful device on the other to incorporate and/or create change. It also places emphasis on the behavioristic, e.g., on the importance of people to the process. It requires the use of the group process and the energy created from the group effort, and depends on good communication, consensus building, openness, and mutual trust (Cargill and Webb 1988; Casserly 1987; Kells 1988; Lindquist 1978; Williams 1983).

Some key factors are described by Kells (1988) and adapted from Lindquist (1978) which are considered important ingredients for change, factors which will help to create the kind of environment within which effective change can occur. The first requirement, again, is a leader or, if you will, a change agent, who will initiate, promote, and facilitate the process. This may or may not be the leader in the traditional sense; however, if it is to be planned change, it will be a leader from within the learning resources center. It will probably be the director, but it may also be a department head or member of the staff who, in bringing forth an idea, is supported by management to implement it, and who is willing to take the responsibility for following through. Studies show that "colleges resist changing academic practices [or LRC practices]; what little change does happen occurs more by external pressure than internal plan" (Lindquist p. 15). That kind of external pressure creates a kind of change with which we are all familiar: wrenching, most always resisted, and when accepted or adopted, usually begrudgingly. That result may be change, but it will certainly not be effective. The response from the LRC staff is likely to be that the change that has occurred is not the way *they* would have done it had *they* only been in charge. The challenge is, then, to *be* in charge, to plan the change that is inevitable, but to effect it in LRC's own image and not in someone else's version of it. Therefore, planned change is intended and led (and inspired, if we are lucky), and it uses such practices as self-study and planning to accomplish its mission.

A second factor in the change process is the linking of people to ideas. As with self-study and planning, it is the people who make the process—or break it. And in academe in general, as Lindquist reminds us, and specifically in the library and learning resources center, people are resistant to change. New ideas need to be germinated and new attitudes and behaviors need to be created, and it is not likely to happen without raising the awareness, interest, and knowledge level of the LRC staff. Because we are both social and intellectual beings, in order to change and, therefore, grow, we all need to interact with "opinion leaders and reference groups . . . through social [and professional] networks" (Lindquist p. 12). That can best be accomplished when the staff are purposefully linked, or exposed, to new and innovative ideas and practices. This may be accomplished through research and study; through travel to professional meetings, seminars or other LRC facilities; and through inviting visitors and experts onto campus to instruct and demonstrate within one's own LRC setting.

The other factors impacting on the LRC's ability to effect change are motivation, openness of process, and ownership. The fact that we are all also psychological beings, who have fears of the unknown and reasons to protect our own vested interests, needs to be accounted for. More than just the "impressive messages or social influences" (Lindquist p. 12) of the experts with whom staff may have been engaged in the linking process will be needed to persuade most of them that change can indeed be a good thing. The main obstacles to change may boil down to the way staff are treated and invited to participate in the process.

While rarely is anything conducted in secret in the learning resources center (in fact, in my LRC, the informal grapevine is so good that I have come to use it myself for getting information out to the troops in emergency situations), important, need-to-know information often may not get to the individuals who should have it, and have it early in the process. Inadvertent as that may indeed be, staff can (and will) get anxious—or worse, distrustful—when there is the appearance of events that will affect them without their knowledge. There is no surer way to build in failure for a new idea or venture. Whatever the process or project, then, creating and maintaining open channels of communication among all parties is essential—having meetings, writing memos, making phone calls, posting notices, publishing newsletters or updates, etc. The more open the process, the greater the trust; the more open the process, the less likely staff will be apprehensive, and the more likely they will be to take part willingly and to work for and allow change to happen.

In his planning model, Mackenzie, too, focuses on the importance of motivating and rewarding staff throughout the process. Many of the ways that one can motivate and reward staff can be informal and simple—a brief note, a phone call, a private word in passing, or better yet, a word of praise in a public forum. More formal measures should also be employed, such as letters of recognition to supervisors or to personnel files, and, where and if possible, monetary or in-kind awards that allow for travel or study. Also incumbent on the LRC manager in motivating staff is the recognition of the amount of time it takes for these things to happen, coupled with the patience to allow it to happen.

Last, but not least, of the factors necessary for effective planned change is the need to create a sense of ownership in the LRC staff. Staff members who have fully participated in the planning, problem solving, and decision making inherent in the creation and implementation of a new service, idea, or program are those most likely to promote and support it. If they have engaged in all of the discussions of the problems and of the alternatives, they will be committed to the solutions and see them as their own—they will have "bought in."

Conclusion

The intention here has been to describe the interrelationships among self-study, planning, and change. These processes are indispensable management tools to assist with the assessment and accountability requirements placed on those who manage in institutions of higher education today. The effective learning resources center manager in the 1990's will need to understand and employ these processes in order to identify, develop, provide, and evaluate effective and relevant information services; to demonstrate their importance and usefulness to the educational mission of the college; and to compete within the institution for the resources it will need to achieve that. Integral to this notion of LRC effectiveness is also the ability to engage the professional and support staff productively in the achievement of that mission through their active involvement at every stage in the process.

Bibliography

Adams, Mignon. "Developing College Library Leaders of Tomorrow." *College and Research Libraries News* 50.7 (1989): 573–74.

The American Heritage Dictionary of the English Language, ed. William Morris, 1976, s.v. "planning."

Breivik, Patricia Senn. "Making the Most of Libraries: In the Search for Academic Excellence." *Change* July–Aug. 1987: 44–52.

Cargill, Jennifer, and Gisela M. Webb. *Managing Libraries in Transition.* Phoenix: Oryx Press, 1988.

Casserly, Mary. "Accreditation-Related Self-Study as a Planned Change Process: Factors Relating to Its Success in Academic

Libraries." *Journal of Library Administration* Spring 1987: 85–105.

Cross, K. Patricia (Elizabeth and Edward Conner Professor of Higher Education, University of California, Berkeley). "Helping Teachers Improve Learning." Paper Presented to the Annual Conference of the National Council for Staff, Program and Organizational Development. Columbia, Maryland. November 5, 1989.

Ewell, Peter T. "Assessment: Where Are We? The Implications of New State Mandates." *Change* Jan.–Feb. 1987: 23–28.

Finn, Chester E. "Judgement Time for Higher Education: In the Court of Public Opinion." *Change* July–Aug. 1988: 35–39.

Kalick, Rosanne. "Another World at End of the Fishing Line." Editorial. Westchester County Opinion Section. *New York Times* 20 Aug. 1989: 28.

Kania, Antoinette M. "Academic Library Standards and Performance Measures." *College and Research Libraries* Jan. 1988: 16–23.

———. "Self-Study Methods for the Library and Learning Resources Center." *New Directions for the Community College.* Vol. 71. San Francisco: Jossey-Bass, 1990. 81–90. 1973– .

Kells, H. R. "Self-Study Processes." 3rd ed. American Council on Education/Macmillan Series on Higher Education. New York: Macmillan, 1988.

Koenig, Michael E. D., and Leonard Kerson. "Strategic and Long Range Planning in Libraries and Information Centers." *Advances in Library Administration and Organization.* Vol. 2. Greenwich, Conn.: JAI Press, 1983. 199–258. 1982– .

Lindquist, Jack. *Strategies for Change.* Santee, Calif.: Pacific Soundings Press, 1978.

Mackenzie, R. Alec. "The Management Process in 3-D." *Harvard Business Review* Nov.–Dec. 1969: 80–87.

McClure, Charles R. "Library Planning: A Status Report." *ALA Yearbook of Library and Information Services.* Vol. 11. Chicago: American Library Association, 1986. 7–16. 1984– .

Moore, Kay McCullough. "Assessment of Institutional Effectiveness." *New Directions for the Community College.* Vol. 56. San Francisco: Jossey-Bass, 1986. 49–60. 68 vols. to date. 1973– .

Moran, Barbara. *Academic Libraries: The Changing Knowledge Centers of Colleges and Universities.* ASGE-ERIC Higher Education Research Reports 8. Washington, D.C.: Association for the Study of Higher Education, 1984; Washington, D.C.: Clearinghouse on Higher Education, 1984.

Spangehl, Stephen D. "The Push to Assess: Why It's Feared and How to Respond." *Change* Jan.–Feb. 1987: 35–39.

Stueart, Robert D., and Barbara B. Moran. *Library Management.* 3rd ed. Englewood, Calif.: Libraries Unlimited, 1987.

Williams, Delmus E. "Evaluation and the Process of Change in Academic Libraries." *Advances in Library Administration and Organization.* Vol. 2. Greenwich, Conn.: JAI Press, 1983. 151–74. 1982–.

EXCELLENCE AT THE URBAN COMMUNITY COLLEGE LIBRARY

Ngozi P. Agbim

If one were to dare a summary pronouncement of the overall primary mission of the community college, one would say that it is to provide access and quality educational opportunity for all persons. This involves and, at one and the same time, explains its open-door policy and the resultant diverse student population which it attracts.

The enrollment demographics in the urban community college are vastly diversified in terms of racial and ethnic composition, in terms of culture, in terms of academic preparedness, and in terms of primary objectives for attending. There are more women, more older students, more part-timers, more disabled students, and more immigrants. This element of cultural diversity becomes the key factor distinguishing the urban institution from its non-urban counterpart.

Minorities and foreigners constitute a very large proportion of the student body. This phenomenon is mainly due to the fact that "ethnic and racial minorities are heavily urbanized. 83% of all Hispanics, 77% of all Blacks, and 80% of all Asian Americans live in urban areas" (American Association of Community and Junior Colleges 1988, 5). According to the City University of New York (CUNY) student population statistics of fall 1988, its seven community colleges with a total student enrollment of 58,256 have an ethnic distribution as follows: 28.9% white; 35.7% black; 28.2% Hispanic; 1.5% Native American, and 5.7% Asian (Hyman 1988/1989, 66). At my own institution, LaGuardia Community College, 16.2% of students are white, 36% black, 37.9% Hispanic, 2.1% Native American, and 7.8% Asian (Hyman 1988/1989, 66). Also at LaGuardia, foreign students, who make up 9.1% of the total full-time enrollment, come from 73 countries speaking 45 different languages and "enriching the college environment with more than 100 different cultures" (LaGuardia Community College, Foreign Students Office 1990, 1).

In addition, the urban community college, in an attempt to serve the educational needs of its immediate community, maintains very close links with area high schools. In the case of LaGuardia, two Board of Education experimental high schools are actually resident at the campus and share a variety of college facilities, resources, and personnel. The older of these schools, Middle College High School (M.C.H.S.), was established in 1974 with an initial enrollment of 117 "at-risk" students who were very likely drop-out candidates from high schools in western Queens. Now, 15 years later, M.C.H.S. is still going strong, graduating 440 students annually, 80% of whom go to college. Fortified by its success with the M.C.H.S., LaGuardia entered into another joint venture with the Board of Education in 1985 to found the International High School (I.H.S.), enrolling only foreign-born students who have been in the country not more than four years. This experiment has also been crowned with great successes. But what is pertinent about all this is that these high schools, although they have their own regular Board of Education teachers, have neither their own library nor librarian(s). They are both served by the LaGuardia Community College Library, and library staff and faculty.

In recent years, the urban community college more than any other institution of higher education is faced with the challenge of identifying strategies for improving the academic achievement of its diverse student population. Although many students, especially in the 1970s and 1980s, originally enrolled in career programs leading to two-year terminal degrees resulting in immediate employment, many faculty members as well as students are discovering that the current "surplus of baccalaureate graduates is making community college graduates unemployable in fields such as accounting and computer science, where jobs were once regarded as well within reach of two-year college graduates" (Richardson and Bender 1987, 39). Thus, the urban community college is under pressure not only to provide effective remedial programs for its largely underprepared students but to prepare these students for gainful employment and/or successful transfer to senior colleges. Therefore, "the search continues for strategies that offer some chance of improving student success without violating the community college commitment to open access" (Richardson and Bender 1987, 61).

The challenges confronting the urban community college library are implicit in the above mission and challenges of its parent institution. The library's quest for excellence therefore resides in two key areas: (*a*) in its ability to devise creative ways of executing its traditional functions in order to meet the challenges of the changing curricula, the changing methodologies of instruction delivery, the changing technologies of the information age, and the unique needs of the urban student; (*b*) in its ability to initiate change in what and how students learn by playing campus politics and reinforcing its teaching role.

The collection must be multi-formatted in nature and must include resources in a variety of comprehension levels to cater to the needs of its diverse primary clientele and to support reasonably its multi-faceted curriculum offerings. At LaGuardia Community College, for example, the library collection supports the entire high school curriculum. In addition to close liaison work with the M.C.H.S. and I.H.S. teachers, we also use certain basic collection development tools, such as: Baker and Taylor, *School Selection Guide '90: Recommended Books for School Libraries, Grades 7–12;* Friedberg, Joan B., et al., *Accept Me as I Am: Best Books of Juvenile Nonfiction on Impairments and Disabilities;* Hillegas, Ferne E., and Juliette Yaskov, eds., *Senior High School Library Catalog,* 13th ed.; LiBretto, Ellen V., *High/Low Handbooks: Books, Materials and Services for the Problem Reader,* 2nd ed.; Nakamura, Joyce, ed., *High Interest Books for Teens: A Guide to Book Reviews and Biographical Sources,* 2nd ed.

Furthermore, a small but very actively utilized children's collection caters to the immediate needs of the campus day-care program, without which many female students could not stay in college.

Many urban academic institutions, especially the comprehensive community colleges, establish cooperative education systems by which they enter into partnerships with metropolitan businesses. These companies and organizations provide experiential learning in terms of internships (paid or volunteered) for the students. LaGuardia has been noted as the only community college in the nation which requires all its full-time students to participate in cooperative education programs. This obliges the student to acquire three quarters of internship experience, including three 7-week seminars, for a total of nine co-op credits.

To support this special program, the library not only collects heavily in the area of cooperative and experimental education, but it also maintains the Central Employer Resource File (CERF), vertical files of brochures, annual reports, and other documents about the companies and organizations in which our students intern. The Library Media Center and its television studio provide internship experience for many students every year. The library faculty participate in simulated interview programs for students preparing for work interviews. The CERF comes in quite handy at this time. Some library faculty also teach as adjuncts, conducting the Co-op Seminars in which students try to reinforce the relationship between the classroom experience and the world of work.

Additional sections of the collection contain high-interest, low-reading-level tools to support the adult literacy program and numerous non-credit offerings of a large continuing education division. Most of these titles are duplicated and housed in the adult literacy department laboratory for quick and easy access to adult learners.

Bearing in mind that ours is a commuter institution, the reserve section includes all textbooks currently in use in all courses. Needless to say, the students greatly appreciate the service. We feel that learning should continue even when the student forgets the textbook at home or office.

Although the continuous budgetary constraints make it impossible for any library to be self-sufficient, the urban academic library must endeavor to build and maintain a strong reference collection. It is all right, for instance, to subscribe to many relevant general and subject indexes even when the periodical titles held by the library are not nearly adequate to support the indexes. This situation provides a welcome opportunity for urban faculty and students, usually pressed for time, to locate at the home campus bibliographic citations needed for research or a project. Once this process is complete, collecting the appropriate data becomes easier. They may be interloaned, or faxed, or the user may be easily referred to appropriate other collection(s) in the city. Moreover, experience has shown that many urban community college students are not too eager to venture out into unfamiliar ground. Negotiating the mysterious environment of one library is problem enough.

Certain aspects of library services are obviously affected by the urban location of the academic library. There is always a shortage of space and lots of students. The library is always shifting or moving one section or the other in order to make room for one more CD-ROM station, some other new service, or more seating for students. Reference queries revolve around the usual hot issues of child abuse, battered wives, abortion, capital punishment, euthanasia, and other problems which seem to form the bulk of research topics emanating from the urban community college classroom. Reference librarians are experiencing burnout from a repetitious explanation of the *Readers' Guide* and other basic reference tools. The community college campus, like the city, never sleeps. Following in its parent institution's footsteps, the library maintains long service hours, including weekends, in order to accommodate the needs of its extended day and weekend-only population. This has implications for staffing. The library director and the personnel committee must engage in recruitment efforts that yield dependable, creative, and resourceful professional and support staff especially interested in and disposed to, due to their particular circumstances, working evening and weekend shifts on a permanent basis. Fortunately, the urban environment is usually rich in a variety of human resources, and it is usually possible to find desired candidates by tapping into the highly heterogeneous urban labor pool.

The prevailing scarcity of time in the urban environment is an issue which should be taken into consideration in planning strategies for effective library services for faculty and students. As Barbara Dunlap aptly observed, "The most distinguishing feature of being an urban student—and the one which impacts the most on our work—is that one is always rushing, always needing to be somewhere else in twenty minutes: a class, a writing lab, a job or the day care center" (1989, 26). Some ideas of service come to mind. Public service functions must be accentuated and included in every librarian's job description (even in technical services), thus making each librarian a generalist and one who, as much as possible, has the opportunity to deal directly with the primary clientele of the college. Simplify and routinize as many tasks as possible. In this age of library automation, cataloging, for example, must be simple, quick, and orderly. Much original cataloging should be avoided. Most copy cataloging, automated-acquisition-system operations (including the consequent bookkeeping and statistical production), and answering of directional and simple ready-reference questions should be assigned to well-trained paraprofessionals. From the outset, the library director must clarify lines of demarcation for all staff in order to save time for more pressing professional services.

The reference staff must be knowledgeable about resources, services, and access policies of the wider information arena within and outside its own campus. It must be involved in local and regional consortia meetings and continuing education programs in order to maintain needed contacts with peers in the surrounding environment, for although many urban community college students may be reluctant, or too busy with other commitments, to venture out into the unknown, the faculty have less difficulty traveling to relevant information sources to fulfill their research needs.

In serving the students at the reference desk, the rule of thumb should be to take nothing for granted. Many students come ill-equipped to handle the complex academic library system either because, as Dunlap noted, they were used to the "minimumly-stocked" urban high school library or they are foreign students whose library service experience, if any, totally differs from the practice here in the United States (Dunlap 1989, 28). Tell the student what, how, and where to look but keep a vigilant eye on the individual's progress, and quickly come to the rescue if you perceive the need for extra help, and more important, whenever possible, allay the student's fear by directing him/her to a useful source which can provide some answers to the problem at hand. Devise some step-saving mechanism to enable the reference librarian to remain at the reference desk while at the same time directing the student to the appropriate stack aisle or the catalog. At LaGuardia, we have a plan of the open-stacks system on the reference desk showing the aisle markings and numbers, so that looking at the call number of the material sought by the user, the librarian can automatically give the aisle number in which the material is located. In like manner, using the COM catalog at the reference desk, the librarian can tell the user which fiche color and number to use in order to locate the catalog citation for a needed title. These and many other coping tricks are invaluable at the busy urban community college reference desk, which cannot afford to have more than one reference librarian on duty at the same time even during peak periods.

A valuable time-saving service for faculty may be built into the design of the library collection data base during retrospective conversion. The vendor could be asked to allow extra local fields to enable the library to produce, as needed or at faculty request, a printout of major resources in each individual field studied at the college. This type of list is especially valuable for an instructor proposing a new course, writing a grant proposal, or developing a new program.

The library may also offer faculty the current contents of key journals in their fields on a regular basis to make it easier for them to keep up to date with developments in their disciplines (Herring 1988, 47–48).

All librarians must do reference work as well as their special duties, but the head of reference has the responsibility to create a supportive atmosphere at the reference desk. He/she must see him/herself not only as someone who works several hours per week on the desk but, more important, as one who oversees and supports action on the library floor, and tries to bring about the needed library-classroom partnership to foster easy access to information. For example, a memorandum or a flyer should go out at the beginning of each quarter or semester offering professional library assistance to faculty interested in designing and integrating library-related assignments into their courses. The flyer should also solicit copies of all library-dependent projects emanating from the classroom for deposition at the reference desk so that the library faculty scheduled there may be prepared to help students faster and more efficiently. Wherever appropriate, sources or aid files should be created for ease in handling difficult as well as often-asked questions. For the urban community college student nothing promotes learning so much as the discovery that not only the classroom instructor but also the lab technician, the tutor, the counselor, and the reference librarian are interested in, and actually know, the class assignment or project.

Given the predominance of the diversity of students in the urban community college, the institution places great emphasis on instruction. The library, having been upgraded since the early 1970's to the Learning Resource Center (LRC) status, is poised to make a significant contribution to educational life and play a major leadership role in the effort to improve instruction. But herein lies one of the major challenges facing the library. There's always a tendency to exclude it from the mainstream of academic innovations, and to pay only lip service to its being the nerve center of the academic institution. "In a recent book on excellence in the community college, not a single chapter is devoted to the library or the learning resource center. Two paragraphs on communication mention the flow of information between both individuals and groups, but the library is not included. Nor is the library included in the Roueche-Baker Community College Excellence model" (Dale 1988, 237).

A study of the teaching/learning process in an urban community college by Richard C. Richardson reported a decline in student reading and writing of connected prose. Rather, the student is expected to give back, via multiple-text mode, bits of information culled from the instructor's handouts and/or lectures, thus fostering student dependence on the instructor as opposed to becoming an independent learner (1985, 43–44). This type of student and instructor will obviously not see the need for library research. This situation can be turned around by planned, concentrated, sustained, and patient effort on the part of the library faculty.

The library must be alert to and involved with any institutional programs connected with the current wave of curricular reform in higher education in general. In the urban community college, this has assumed a particularly stressful stance due to great diversity in its student preparation and student objectives. The pressure is on for the urban community college to foster the academic success of its non-traditional student. Types of academic reforms under consideration run the gamut from orientation-program revivals, to renewal of team-taught interdisciplinary courses, to writing across the curriculum, to core or general education requirements, to integration of curriculum for multi-cultural education. Whichever it is, the library must consistently and effectively be represented at the planning stages of any programs for change. Librarians need to make it clear "that libraries do have much to offer in the addressing of identified educational priorities and that library personnel and resources can be strong tools of empowerment for achieving those priorities" (Breivik 1989, 13).

Multi-cultural education has been a major educational priority at LaGuardia recently. The library's involvement took several directions. We sought for and obtained representation in an important institutional "Pluralism Task Force" established by the president to coordinate all activities—including lectures and workshops—pertaining to the project. The library quickly became the clearinghouse for all pertinent information generated by various multi-cultural education-related programs. During the annual faculty development week held in September 1990, the library had a panel presentation entitled "Pluralism in the Curriculum: A Review of Literature." The panelists discussed examples, culled from current literature, of curriculum integration efforts for pluralism undertaken at select academic institutions across the nation. We also seized the opportunity to demonstrate excerpts from our media and videodisc collections that can be utilized to introduce multi-cultural issues into courses or programs. Both administration and faculty who attended felt that this library initiative was an excellent one and would be very helpful in translating the idea of pluralism into concrete instructional action.

Now, more than ever, the teaching role of the urban community college library must be expanded to include formal participation of the library in the team-taught interdisciplinary courses as well as in credit-bearing information literacy courses which fulfill liberal arts or other requirements for graduation. Given the current major trends in community college education, the challenges and demands made upon this institution by its counterparts in the four-year colleges and universities, by the accrediting bodies, by the funding agencies, and by the potential employers of its graduates, the library should seek a more formal, predictable, and stable form of involvement in solving the educational problems of our day. In a speech recently delivered to librarians and academic deans by the new executive director of the Middle States Commission on Higher Education, bibliographic instruction is emphasized as one of the major elements to be considered by the commission in the academic institutional accreditation process (Simmons 1989).

In the urban community college, one can begin with any group within the diverse student body (adult students, immigrants, high school population, students in remedial programs, etc.) or with an issue (basic skills or general education, for example) that touches the majority or all of the students and demonstrates the relevant application of the information literacy program to the group or issue.

I strongly recommend the addition of a credit-bearing, required information-literacy course to every community college library-user-education program. At LaGuardia Community College, the instructional program of the library includes a 3-credit liberal arts elective course (LRC102, "Information Strategies") taught by the library faculty. Many students who have taken this course ask why it is not a required course for all students. Contrary to some opinions in library literature, students enrolled in "Information Strategies" are quite able, with ease, to transfer skills acquired in the course to other courses which they are taking concurrently and to future programs. We also find that we don't have to lobby the fiscal officers for the necessary funding to run this course; once there are enough students enrolled, it is automatically funded. This is because the college administration understands full-time-equivalents (FTEs) more than they do libraries. Credit-bearing courses bring in FTEs and are therefore happily funded. The library faculty feel that in teaching this course, they have more academic freedom and the most desirable opportunity actually to demystify the modern complex library for students, thus liberating them from the shackles of information illiteracy and promoting lifelong learning.

Although student recruitment into a formal library course always poses a problem, the key to success is to work patiently with the curriculum committee, the academic chairs and other governance bodies on the campus to obtain a liberal arts elective or required status for the course. Then proceed to making presentations to the counselors who provide advice to students during registration. With the chair of the Library Department in the lead, the library faculty should be visible at the registration area at scheduled periods, pass out flyers, and explain the value of the course to the students as they prepare for registration.

Finally, if the course runs, use a little imagination. Put the library's television studio to good use. Videotape members of the class discussing the value of the library course for future enrollees. Edit down the program to a manageable size. Dub in appropriate music and add titles and graphics. This makes a powerful recruiting tool for future classes. Before you know it, students will be talking to other students, and the recruitment problem will be greatly reduced.

All in all, the urban community college library does not have to go far to find its path to excellence. It just needs to get actively involved in meeting the challenges of fulfilling the mission of its parent institution, carrying out its teaching role, and other traditional functions with a lot of imagination, creativity, and flexibility—a sure path to excellence.

References

American Association of Community and Junior Colleges, Report of the Urban Community Colleges Commission. *Minorities in Urban Community Colleges: Tomorrow's Students Today.* Washington, D.C.: National Center for Higher Education, 1988.

Breivik, Patricia Senn. "Politics for Closing the Gap," in *Integrating Library Use Skills into the General Education Curriculum,* edited by Maureen Pastine and Bill Katz. New York: Haworth Press, 1989.

Dale, Doris Cruger. "The Learning Resource Center's Role in the Community College System," *College and Research Libraries,* May 1988: 232–238.

Dunlap, Barbara. "The Essence of Urban Academic Librarianship," *Urban Academic Librarian,* Fall 1988/Spring 1989: 25–29.

Herring, Mark Y. "The Two-Year College Library," in *The How to Do It Manual for Small Libraries,* edited by Bill Katz. New York, Neal-Schuman Publishers, 1988.

Hyman, Richard Joseph. "Libraries in the City University of New York—Adaptations in Cataloging and Classification." *Urban Academic Librarian,* Fall 1988/Spring 1989: 58–66.

LaGuardia Community College, Foreign Students Office. "If You Look Closely Enough at LaGuardia You Can See the Whole World," *Microcosm,* Winter 1990.

Richardson, Richard C. "How Are Students Learning?" *Change,* May/June 1985.

Richardson, Richard C., Jr., and Louis W. Bender. "The Urban Community College's Role in Educating Minorities," in *Fostering Minority Access and Achievement in Higher Education.* San Francisco: Jossey-Bass Publishers, 1987.

Simmons, Howard L. "An Accreditor's Perspective: Bibliographic Instruction as a Tool for Learning," Borough of Manhattan Community College, City University of New York, May 19, 1989.

COMMUNITY COLLEGE LIBRARIES: ELECTRONIC BRIDGES TO RURAL AMERICA'S FUTURE

Edwin F. Rivenburgh

A walk through the fields of the countryside still provides beauty and solitude. Today, however, tall metal towers rise in counterpoint above the pastoral landscape. Antennae simultaneously receive hundreds of microwave and cellular telephone messages, amplify and transmit them to the next tower. The fields may also be filled with patterns of numbered stakes soon to guide huge earth-moving vehicles as they carve out homes, roads, swimming pools, and golf courses of another condominium complex. Such development sites provide tangible evidence of the migratory phenomenon bringing a historically urban-based population back to rural America.

Population migration from the country to the city is a major theme of United States history. Particularly during the nineteenth and early twentieth centuries, the city lured many with the promise of better paying, industrial-based jobs and the excitement of living where the benefits of the Industrial Revolution were most in evidence. Commerce, with its insatiable need for better transportation, communication, and education systems, was a driving force in this industrialization process. These systems, combined with the large, permanent, urban populations and constant flow of visitors, also encouraged development of major arts and entertainment centers.

An important component of the urban milieu was the collection, organization, mass storage, and utilization of centralized information. Cities became the information repositories needed to operate the nation's political, financial, legal, educational, and medical "industries." Under manual, paper-based information systems, access to highly centralized, physical documents stored in urban centers was a critical requirement for successful operation and growth of those organizations.

Urban centers now exact a heavy toll from their inhabitants. High crime rates fueled by an extensive illegal drug economy, automotive and aircraft gridlock, inadequate housing, dangerous air pollution, and widespread poverty are but a few of the indicators that the promise of the affluent urban lifestyle has, instead, frequently led people to profound alienation from environment, neighbor, and self.

As a result, Americans are returning to rural settings. The United States Bureau of the Census reports the population of small rural American towns increased annually by over two million during the seventies. The migration to the city that permeated American history has virtually ceased. Census Bureau figures capture this cessation:

	% Urban Population	% Increase
1890	35.1 %	24.5 %
1900	39.6 %	12.8 %
1910	45.6 %	15.2 %
1920	51.2 %	12.3 %
1930	56.1 %	9.6 %
1940	56.5 %	0.7 %
1950	64.0 %	13.3 %
1960	69.9 %	9.2 %
1970	73.6 %	5.3 %
1980	73.7 %	0.1 %

Source: Hacker (24).

These figures are particularly significant since the Census Bureau here defines "urban" as any city, town, or village having more than 2,500 residents. As soon as rural localities obtain any sizable population, they are redefined out of existence.

The emergence of job opportunities is a major reason people can now relocate to rural environs. Demographers Larry Long and Diana DeAre note, "In some regions and in some industries, the rate of growth [in the 1970's] in jobs was far greater in rural counties than it was in metropolitan counties" (37). The new rural work force is taking form as service and information-based businesses replace heavy industrial manufacturing. Proliferation of efficient international delivery systems permits much less reliance on proximity to raw materials in the production of today's goods. Long-term tax breaks provided through rural economic development programs also encourage company relocation. Many companies are finding they must build their research and industrial parks in a rural environment to attract the quantity and quality of workers needed to compete in an international market economy. Employers know many professional and technical employees want to work, live, and raise families in a non-urbanized setting.

This movement back to the countryside is not based on an unrealistic desire to "return to the land." These rural homesteaders are not modern Thoreaus, wishing to dissociate themselves from the world and their neighbors. They are ready and able to engage the modern world on its own terms, but want the physical and psychic benefits of the rural experience—benefits which include reasonably priced housing, freedom from pervasive crime, and a healthy, clean physical environment. They also, however, seek the same employment opportunities, rewards, and access to professional resources found within the urban setting. Long and DeAre conclude from their research, "The new rural demographic concentrations appear to represent small centers of urban culture transplanted to the countryside and enabled to survive by recent advances in communications, transportation and methods of industrial production" (38).

This recent concentration of population and importation of the "urban culture" to rural America is having tremendous repercussions. The need for improved public services frequently outpaces increases in the local tax base. Property costs climb beyond reach of longtime residents. Condominium tracts deface forests and wetlands before municipalities can adopt appropriate master plans and zoning regulations. In short, urban migration to rural settings has already demonstrated a capacity to destroy that which it seeks. Careful municipal planning and development of controlled-growth strategies are necessary if the benefits of country living are to be shared—not eliminated.

The resettlement of rural America is possible only because

technology—particularly modern telecommunications and computer informations systems—has drastically reduced the deficiency of employment-related opportunities and resources historically associated with rural life. Access to information is a critical requirement for successful transplantation of a significant segment of our urban-based population into rural environments. The over five hundred community college libraries found in rural settings across the nation are uniquely positioned to respond effectively to this need.

Many community college libraries have as a part of their mission meeting the information needs not only of their students and faculty but also of local community residents. Until recently, however, providing access to information resources that adequately supported even the formal curricula, much less the diverse information needs of the community at large, was a difficult task. Many rural community college libraries have been forced to address their dual mission of serving the college and the community with too few staff members, inadequate budgets, and limited in-house collections. Providing effective access to information beyond their own collections has been impossible.

The overwhelming nature of the mission they faced and the inadequacy of available resources frequently created an environment within the rural community college library where excellence in service seemed unobtainable. Dedicated librarians had to live daily with so many compromises in the service they were able to provide that survival sometimes became a stronger motivating force than striving toward excellence. A service orientation grounded in scarcity rarely brings forth the vision or energy required to develop active outreach programs. There was inadequate time for long-range planning or implementation of new services. Available energy had to be focused on supporting the hour-by-hour, course-related needs of students and faculty, a very important but frequently undervalued and low-visibility activity within the college community.

Despite their rhetoric, too many community college administrators, and even faculty, viewed the library as a component required but tangential to the college's main mission—classroom instruction. Librarians lacked the resources needed to improve access to information and expand their mission into areas of increased importance to community colleges, including participation in the community's economic-development programs and implementation of formal educational partnerships with local school systems.

This negative cycle frequently fed upon itself. Community college administrators and trustees constantly faced tremendous demands from throughout the college for their limited fiscal resources. Based upon their perception of the librarian's role and activities, frequently grounded in the historical repository model, they sometimes saw additional library funding as providing only a few more books and magazines on shelves.

College administrators, and unfortunately some librarians, failed to see the potential for their libraries to become among the most critical resources on campus and among the most effective lifelong learning laboratories. To reach such a goal requires a paradigm shift away from the isolated book-warehouse viewpoint toward a vision of the rural community college library as an exciting, electronic gateway capable of identifying and retrieving required information from extensive knowledge networks around the world, while minimizing the determinants of location, space, time, and distance that have historically prohibited such access.

Technology now offers rural community college libraries the capacity to expand dramatically the range and improve the quality of information services available to their students, faculty, and community residents. They can now serve a clientele increasingly diverse and demanding in their information requirements. Community college libraries can, with sufficient vision and commitment, play a critical role in creating rural communities where people may live, work, and play in a life-affirming setting without sacrificing access to information essential for success in an uncertain, challenging global environment.

Accomplishing this goal will require some rural community colleges and their libraries to commit significantly greater effort and resources toward serving the information needs of their local communities. Most important, however, rural community college administrators, trustees, faculty, and sometimes even library personnel must first recognize and then financially support technology's tremendous potential to

transform radically their libraries into comprehensive information resource centers capable of meeting the diverse and
complex information needs of both campus and community
in this Postindustrial Age.

In 1975, the National Commission on Libraries and Information Science (NCLIS) issued the document *Toward a National Program for Library and Information Services: Goals for
Action*. That commission succinctly identified the following
as its major goal:

> To eventually provide every individual in the United
> States with equal opportunity to that part of the total
> information resources which will satisfy the individual's
> educational, working, cultural, and leisure-time needs
> and interests regardless of the individual's location, so-
> cial, physical condition or level of intellectual achieve-
> ment. [Introduction xi]

This powerful statement on the necessity of providing equal
access must have certainly struck a responsive chord in many
rural community college librarians, who recognized the need
and struggled for so many years to bring about such a reality.
While understanding the intrinsic value of their rural environment, they remained painfully aware of their inability to
provide information resources needed to navigate through
the modern world. The rural community college librarian had
very limited bibliographic or physical access to the collections
of large academic, public, medical, or industrial libraries. In
addition, information contained in computer data bases was
available only through highly centralized, expensive, mainframe computers requiring extensive technical training to use
and maintain.

Will we ever appreciate how profoundly that isolationism
was forever shattered by the microchip? Was it really only
fifteen years ago that the first microcomputers began showing
up in electronics stores, and just a few years earlier that a few
libraries in Ohio began to do some common cataloging
through a small cooperative venture, now called OCLC, Inc.?
Even today, not all librarians seem to understand adequately
how microchip-based computer and telecommunications
technology is redefining the historical form and even the
functions of libraries.

Ironically, the effects of this redefinition may presently best be displayed not in large university library systems but rather at the other end of the spectrum, where small, rural community college libraries are being significantly transformed—and empowered—by this technology. Community college librarians are acquiring effective new electronic tools at a time when the successful resettlement of rural America requires retrieval of quantities and types of information on a scale that would have been impossible to provide a few years ago.

To view some of these changes, a case study is offered of a community college library in rural, central New York State, chosen not only because of the writer's familiarity but also because the recent phenomenal growth of communities surrounding the college, due to urban migration, is forcing it to address these changes rapidly. The particular confluence of forces that is bringing about such rapid change and placing such extensive demands on this rural environment and its community college may provide insight to others on what they must soon confront as the "ruralization" of America continues. It is important to note that the technological transformation of the community college library described in this case study is occurring in rural community colleges across the country.

Case Study

The Community College of the Finger Lakes (CCFL) is located in Canandaigua, N.Y., within Ontario County, about twenty miles southeast of Rochester. The college sits in the heart of the beautiful Finger Lakes region. Rolling hills, covered with lush vineyards, surround long, deep lakes carved out by retreating Ice Age glaciers. Farmland and forest checkerboard the countryside.

For over one hundred years, the incredible beauty of this region has drawn many visitors and summer residents. Despite this constant visitor flow, permanent residents have remained solidly grounded in a rural culture. The New York State Thruway, which physically divides Rochester from most of Ontario County, is a visible symbol of the separation between the urban and rural populations. Ontario County was not—and until recently, tried hard not to be—a suburb of Rochester.

Within the last ten years, however, major Rochester-based corporations, including Kodak and Xerox, have built high-tech research and manufacturing plants in Ontario County. Several smaller electronics and computer-based firms have also relocated or established operations in the region. From 1979 to 1987, private-sector jobs in Ontario County increased by 20%. Numerous shopping malls and upscale housing tracts are under construction or already occupied. Construction of a large new high school and enlargement of several other schools is underway in Canandaigua.

At the north end of Canandaigua Lake, construction has begun on an extensive condominium development that includes retail stores, restaurants, marina, and conference center. Six years ago an outdoor amphitheater was built on the community college campus. It is the permanent summer home for the Rochester Philharmonic Orchestra. In addition, each summer many well-known entertainers perform in this impressive outdoor facility.

Good jobs, affordable homes, safe and clean communities, and recreational facilities are available within this still basically rural environment, and many residents remain psychically separated from the urban center of Rochester. In recent years, Ontario County and the city of Canandaigua have both experienced significant population growth. In fact, according to recent Census Bureau figures, Canandaigua is the fastest growing city in New York State. Since 1980 its population has grown 17% to approximately 12,000 residents ("Census Estimates . . .").

The growth of the Community College of the Finger Lakes has paralleled that of the environment that surrounds it. From 1979 to 1989, CCFL's full-time-equivalent (FTE) student body has risen from 1,871 to 2,749. New academic programs have been introduced or significantly expanded, including broadcasting, electrical technology, criminal justice, computer science, travel and tourism administration, and hotel/motel management. A major building project for the main campus and development of extension teaching centers in surrounding communities are under way. An Institute for

Business, Industry and Professional Development was started last year by the college, and has been working hard to keep pace with the demand for employee training from local businesses.

Only through a significant infusion of technology has the Community College of the Finger Lakes Library been able to address the tremendous increase and diversification of information needs that has accompanied this recent growth within the college and local communities. Until the mid-eighties, the library's daily weekday attendance was approximately 600 users. In fall 1989, many weekdays saw over 1,000 people using the library.

Until recently, the CCFL Library staff, as in many other rural community colleges, struggled to break the isolation that frequently prevented them from meeting the information requirements of students, faculty, and community residents. The challenge was to secure the information resources needed to support an ever-growing student body and expanded academic programs with a modest library materials budget that was constantly eroded by substantial annual inflation.

The concept of a library freely loaning resources to other libraries has been a hallmark of American librarianship. Unfortunately, lack of bibliographic and location-determination resources meant that into the early eighties, the only way for CCFL to borrow items from other libraries was through participation in a regional "blind" want-list procedure. A list of needed periodicals and monographs was forwarded to a regional library headquarters, combined with similar lists from other colleges, special, and public libraries, and redistributed to all member libraries. Each library then checked its card catalog for ownership and shelves for availability. This lengthy procedure yielded such unpredictable and delayed results it was used infrequently by CCFL Library staff.

Lacking alternatives, the library relied almost totally on the 50,000-item in-house collection of books, periodicals, and media programs. Even with careful collection development, and very judicious use of the annual materials budget, the library was unable to provide all the resources needed to support the college's increasing number of credit-bearing courses. Using only an in-house collection to meet the wide range of information needs generated by the campus and community was frequently a disappointing endeavor for both researcher and librarian.

Providing CCFL library users with access to computer data base searching services was even more frustrating. The librarian conducted a reference interview with the person needing the data base search. This material then began a circuitous trip through Rochester to Albany where the search was performed by the New York State Library. The results of the search arrived weeks later and were frequently disappointing because lack of direct contact between searcher and requestor prohibited collaboratively "reshaping" the search strategy based upon initial results. Even in the early eighties, it seemed as if the CCFL Library was light-years away from reaching NCLIS's goal of providing equal access. The combination of small size and distance from urban-based resources confounded staff efforts toward service excellence.

Compare the above description with current daily activity in the CCFL Library. A student is searching for periodical articles on a research topic using an index installed on a microcomputer connected to CD-ROM drives. Each CD-ROM disc has a storage capacity of approximately 450 megabytes of information. The printed message on the color monitor asks the student to type in words or phrases describing a chosen topic that the microcomputer can use to search in a "free text" mode. Seconds later the computer has searched its large memory banks and is displaying citations to relevant articles and indicating those available in the CCFL Library. Upon command, the microcomputer will also display a synopsis of any cited article. An ink jet printer connected to the microcomputer is used to print out quickly and quietly a list of desired journal articles.

The student then moves to one of several other microcomputers on a nearby table. CD-ROM units are again attached to each microcomputer, but this time the laser discs hold the bibliographic records of CCFL's 60,000 monographs and 4,000 media programs. Supported by a Title IID federal grant, these discs also contain approximately three million records from 13 academic libraries as well as numerous public, school, medical, and industrial libraries in the Rochester region. All these records can be simultaneously searched using Boolean logic and free text. It is easy to limit each search to items available in specified libraries.

One critical outgrowth of the introduction of these new technologies is a requirement for rural community college librarians to teach their users the skills needed to utilize effectively the information retrieval capabilities now available to them. These computer-based research skills have great applicability throughout a society such as ours, where information has become its lifeblood.

To succeed personally and professionally, the clientele of rural community college libraries must gain significant skill and confidence in using these electronic tools. Many community college students transfer to four-year institutions where automated catalogs and other computerized research resources are now commonplace and students are expected to use them effectively.

Introduction of computer-based research tools has already had a profound effect on the amount and type of instruction required to utilize fully the power of the technology. For several years, an arrangement between the CCFL Library staff and the Humanities Department has required every student enrolled in the introductory English course to receive formal library instruction. It was one thing to offer such training when working with an individual small library's card catalog and paper indexes, and quite another challenge when teaching effective operation of CD-ROM periodical indexes and a union computer-based catalog displaying holdings of many libraries.

Data is organized in different formats. Keyboard and "windowed" screen displays replace manually searching through cards in a drawer. The new technology requires learning a new search process. Concepts such as Boolean logic, controlled vs. free-text vocabulary, and truncation must all be taught if the student is to utilize effectively these new research tools.

To offer instruction needed for effective operation of the new computer resources, the CCFL Library staff has developed a multi-phase instructional process. Each student first participates in formal classroom instruction. A library classroom, with a capacity of 40 people, has been renovated to support teaching bibliographic instruction using microcomputers. The librarian uses a movable podium equipped with a microcomputer and CD-ROM drives. The screen display on the librarian's console is projected to a large screen in the front of the room using an overhead projector and a computer-generated projection system. The images are simultaneously displayed in color on monitors mounted on each side of the screen. Carefully designed demonstrations show students how to operate computer equipment located in the library and how to design and execute effective search procedures using the new technology.

Previously, CCFL librarians found many students were not interested in participating in bibliographic instruction activities because they had already "learned that stuff" in high school. While their behavior frequently showed limited knowledge of academic library research methods and resources, the negative attitude they brought to instruction that continued to use the card catalog as its centerpiece was frequently difficult to overcome. CCFL librarians report the natural fascination many students have with microcomputers and their easily demonstrated capacity to locate information students need for research papers quickly and effectively has significantly reduced resistance to the instruction program.

At the end of the classroom instruction each student receives a 60-page workbook with text and exercises detailing effective library research strategy. Selected chapters deal with using the library's computers. Last year over 1,400 students participated in the library-skills workbook program.

The third phase of instruction involves each reference librarian actively monitoring and assisting in use of microcomputer workstations strategically placed near the reference desk. One interesting phenomenon reported by reference librarians is how much more frequently students assist other students to operate the computer workstations than they ever did when using manual indexes or a card catalog. Library users consistently report finding more resources than when they use manual search techniques. Of course, such success also results in heavier use of the library's collection and generates more requests for material held by other libraries.

Armed with printed citations and known locations of material not owned by the CCFL Library, the student goes to the reference desk. A librarian discusses the student's search procedure and examines retrieved citations. The librarian can easily provide the student with additional information by using a microcomputer on the reference desk connected to a modem and phone line. All CCFL librarians can now search large computer data bases from vendors such as DIALOG, BRS, and OCLC. Although these data bases are stored on very large mainframe computers located hundreds or thousands of miles from CCFL, they can deliver needed information to the CCFL reference librarian within seconds after transmittal of the request. These services permit librarians to find information quickly on a cost-effective basis that would have taken many hours or been impossible to locate using manual indexes. Many of these data bases are either not available in a paper format or prohibitively expensive.

Through microcomputer and telecommunications technology, the CCFL Library now provides library users with a tremendous ability to find bibliographic and location information on desired resources. However, bibliographic or "logical" access without easy physical access to those resources is of little value. Fast retrieval of identified documents is a critical requirement for breaking through the isolation barriers that have for so many years limited the effectiveness of rural community college libraries.

In the CCFL Library, requests for documents not available in-house are now met through several avenues. Library staff frequently use the OCLC interlibrary loan sub-system to identify and place requests to specific libraries with needed resources. They search first in the Rochester region and then, if needed, across the country. A daily van delivery system, administered by the Rochester Regional Library Council (RRLC), transports hundreds of books, photocopies, and media programs to Rochester-area libraries. In addition, last year the CCFL Library obtained a telefacsimile machine. The library now transmits and receives copies of requested articles, reports, etc., from other libraries and commercial document vendors throughout the nation.

Another source of material available for loan is through a locally created multi-library system operating in Ontario and Wayne counties. Several years ago the CCFL Library staff played a major role in obtaining competitive grants from New York State, administered by RRLC. The grants allowed creation of a microcomputer-based interlibrary loan system that links the two colleges in Ontario County—Hobart and William Smith Colleges and CCFL—with several public and school libraries in Ontario and Wayne counties. Each participant library now has either CD-ROM discs or a microfiche set containing a union list of the machine-readable holdings of other libraries in the system. Interlibrary loan requests are transmitted daily, usually point to point, using a "home-brew" microcomputer telecommunications system.

CCFL also participates in a cooperative delivery service operated by 25 regional public libraries. Items are delivered among these libraries and CCFL three times each week. CCFL students, who live many miles from the college's main campus, can return CCFL books to any public library in Wayne or Ontario County and have them quickly delivered back to CCFL. CCFL can also efficiently respond to telephone and written requests for monographs and articles from students living far from the campus. The public library system's delivery van transports the needed material to any public library identified by the student. The area's public schools also operate a delivery system using school buses traveling each day from 26 local school districts to a centralized Board of Cooperative Educational Services (BOCES) facility. CCFL utilizes this system to supply books, articles, and media programs requested by public school students, teachers, and administrators.

These delivery systems, coupled with the computerized union list and the microcomputer network, provide rural libraries with logical and physical access to material unavailable just a few years ago. This mini-network permits a rural community college library not only to have access to local collections, but also to play an important role in providing information needed by many users of public and school libraries in nearby rural communities.

The extensive use of microcomputers and telecommunications systems to locate items and place electronic requests has permitted the CCFL Library to offer its many users access to resources previously unknown or inaccessible. During the 1979–80 academic year, the library used a paper-based interlibrary loan system and borrowed 416 items from other libraries. In 1987–88, the library borrowed 1,452 items.

According to figures collected by the State University of New York, CCFL borrowed more that year than any other of the thirty community colleges in the SUNY system. Some may question whether such heavy reliance on interlibrary loan is a wise or even a fair policy. In response, it should be noted that CCFL annually borrows only about 4% of the items it circulates. The college administration continues to demonstrate maintenance of effort by incrementally increasing the serials and book budget each year. Additionally, while in 1979–80, CCFL was a net borrower by a 2 to 1 ratio, the library now loans more items to other libraries than it borrows. For instance, in 1979–80 CCFL loaned only 208 items; by 1987–88 that figure had increased to 1,751.

Most important, rural community colleges are being forced by available technology to rethink how they meet their important dual mission to the college and community. Historically, many rural community college libraries viewed their interlibrary loan operation as a tangential component of their spectrum of services. One important consequence of infusing automation throughout a rural community college library is to force interlibrary loan from the sidelines to the center of information retrieval services. An effective and extensive interlibrary loan service becomes a necessity whenever a library introduces significant on-line and CD-ROM-based reference services. This fact will become even more evident now that OCLC is offering its new subject searching service, EPIC. For the first time the entire OCLC data base of over 20 million items can be searched using techniques similar to searching many CD-ROM products and on-line data base services.

Making the shift from providing library services built on in-house collections to services built around the philosophy of access to information on demand is not always easily accomplished in rural community college libraries, where for years the only way to provide information retrieval services was through the in-house collection. After working for so long in environments permeated by the repository model, it is frequently necessary to make difficult decisions regarding reallocation of funding priorities and staff responsibilities to realize the benefits of library automation. If, however, the goal is to provide needed information in the most cost-effective and timely manner, then frequently the library cannot afford to, and should not want to, purchase physical products.

Often the transition time between manual-based and electronic information retrieval systems is the most difficult. Frequently both systems have to run concurrently during the changeover process, which can be quite lengthy due to fiscal constants. Technology can assist the rural community college librarian even here. For instance, CCFL's heavy participation in interlibrary loan systems has dramatically increased required staff time, yet no funds were available for additional staff. However, by using microcomputers to handle other previously labor-intensive tasks, reallocation of staff responsibilities became a realistic solution. Microcomputers reduce the time needed to produce reports, bibliographies, reserve lists, etc. Budget development and expenditure monitoring are both more efficiently executed through electronic spreadsheets. Overdue notices are automatically generated through a microcomputer software program operating at the circulation desk.

CCFL librarians also used to spend a great deal of time learning the computer commands needed to search an on-line vendor's data base service. Using several services meant learning and remembering several, usually incompatible, command languages. New "front-end" software programs facilitate searching multiple data base vendors with a common command language and significantly reduce both the time needed for staff training and the cost of executing searches (Bell and Rivenburgh 40–48).

It would be hard to overestimate the changes that have occurred since the introduction, in 1983, of microcomputer and telecommunications technology within the CCFL Library. Students and faculty, frequently without assistance, continually and easily locate information that would have been very difficult or impossible to secure, even for our librarians, just a few years ago. CCFL librarians now work closely with faculty members searching out information for their research projects. Previously, an hour drive to libraries in Rochester or Syracuse would have been necessary for faculty to secure the same material.

Hundreds of Ontario County residents take undergraduate

and graduate courses at private and public colleges and universities located many miles from their homes. They continually use the CCFL Library's research services, rather than those offered by the institution in which they are enrolled. They report the CCFL Library now assists them to locate and retrieve needed documents efficiently. Perhaps more important, they report finding our highly service- and community-oriented facility a much more conducive environment in which to do their research. Such comments vividly portray the results of successfully synthesizing the power of library technology with the friendly, communal attitudes frequently engendered by living in a rural environment.

Many more community residents are using the CCFL Library because CCFL's collection is now readily available through CD-ROM and microfiche union lists found throughout community school and public libraries. Whereas a few years ago less than 8% of the library's circulation was attributable to community residents, currently over 20% is generated by residents not attending CCFL classes.

So many high school students from several local school districts have begun using the CCFL Library, and need to learn to take advantage of the electronic research tools, that the library has developed a library instruction program with local public school teachers and librarians. CCFL librarians annually teach over 600 students in twenty-five high school classes, covering language arts, history, and social and natural sciences. The students are accompanied to CCFL by their regular classroom teacher and school librarian. After the classroom instruction, teacher and librarian work with the college librarians to assist students as they use the library's resources.

Technology has also permitted the CCFL Library to serve the community in many other ways. For four years, the library has provided an on-line data base searching service to all residents of Ontario and Wayne counties through a formal arrangement with the regional public and school library systems. Any public or school librarian can call or send through the delivery systems a request for on-line searching services. The public and public school library systems have agreed to pay the first $25 of the search cost, with the requestor paying the rest. Several hundred searches have been successfully completed through this arrangement, which provides mutual benefit to the CCFL Library and the local communities. The local librarians are very appreciative of having this powerful new searching service available so they can better meet the needs of their clients. In exchange, CCFL librarians are enabled continually to improve their searching skills by facing search requests on a challenging array of topics. CCFL librarians currently receive several requests each week for searches from teachers and administrators in local school systems. Some of these requests are now quickly answered, at no cost, by searching the ERIC data base that the CCFL Library has on CD-ROM.

Microcomputers and telecommunications technology is now used by CCFL Library staff to serve the information needs of local industries and businesses. For example, a local farmer needed information about a newly discovered fruit preservation process. A reference librarian located the desired information using on-line data bases. The results were of such great assistance to the farmer that he sent a generous donation to the library's gift fund.

Several local businesses have asked library staff to research such management issues as profit-sharing programs, assessment of employee training methods, and effective executive recruitment techniques. Research into various industrial technologies and trademark problems has also been successfully provided by the library. CCFL librarians met the needs of one business by using commercial data base searching services to identify companies in predesignated geographical markets handling a specified technical product and then produced mailing labels for them. The library's computer-based reference services are currently being offered to local profit and non-profit organizations by the college's new Institute for Business, Industry and Professional Development.

In 1988, a small local law firm was seeking injury compensation for a client from alleged negligence by New York State. The lawyers asked CCFL librarians to locate information on an expert auto accident witness scheduled to testify for the State. Within hours, the librarians had accessed computer data bases across the country to produce a bibliography, with synopses of articles, technical reports, and speeches written by the witness. The library then used electronic interlibrary loan and fax transmissions to retrieve material from all over the country.

The lawyers reported that the wealth of significant material provided by the library helped them to conduct a successful five-hour cross-examination of this key witness. The court recently ruled in their client's favor and issued the largest personal injury judgment against New York State ever awarded in the Court of Claims. The CCFL Library received a gift of several thousand dollars for their assistance.

CCFL librarians have also worked closely with the Ontario County Attorney's Office to provide background research for several cases. Extensive computer searches were conducted on the effects of placing young children on a witness stand in child abuse cases, insurance liability issues on motor vehicle fleets, and determining whether a possibly abused child could have sustained a spiral fracture by getting a leg caught in a crib.

The college has gained positive publicity for the power of its information services because lawyers, businesspeople, and other community leaders talk to their colleagues about the important information services they are now receiving from their community college library—services that were never available to them before in this rural environment. Many new residents are coming to use the services of the CCFL Library after being advised to do so by others in local communities.

Equally important, possessing the electronic tools and training needed to provide important information services competently for diverse community requirements has had a remarkable effect on CCFL librarians. They now have been given the resources needed to meet their professional responsibilities with a high degree of excellence. Offering such opportunities in a rural setting has also proven to be a significant recruiting tool. Highly qualified librarians from larger institutions often see employment in the CCFL Library as offering them access to the challenges and necessary tools of modern librarianship combined with the many benefits of rural living.

It is difficult to overestimate the positive influence this process of technological empowerment of a library can have on its staff. The constant electronic flow of information from one campus library to another, requiring joint staff cooperation, is also creating a stronger sense of common purpose among library professionals. Community college libraries in New York State, many located in rural settings, have in the last few years experienced several demonstrations of collective empowerment engendered by their new technological linkages.

As an example, the political and fiscal structure of the State University of New York, combined with the past isolationism of community college libraries described above, has historically placed these libraries in a very marginal position with regard to determination of SUNY-wide library activities. Community colleges, while operating under both SUNY and local county sponsorship, have been excluded from receiving direct SUNY funding for library services.

A few years ago, library directors from the 13 SUNY Arts and Sciences campuses requested special funding from SUNY that would provide each of their libraries with on-line public access catalogs and circulation systems, and connect these libraries for common resource sharing. Community colleges were going to be excluded from this valuable information network. Community college library directors worked methodically together for over three years to gain SUNY funding for their participation in the SUNY automation project. Community colleges are now full partners in the development and installation of a unified system of automated libraries on SUNY campuses. During the 1990–91 academic year, the first four SUNY campuses were scheduled to receive on-line catalogs and circulation systems under this program—including two community colleges.

Not many years ago, when each community college library operated as an island unto itself, such cooperative action would not have occurred. Inadequate in-house resources and newly gained access to information technologies are forcing community college librarians to recognize the necessity for cooperation and are providing them with strong motivation to influence their professional destiny collectively.

Conclusion

In 1987, New York State issued a pivotal long-range planning document, *Libraries and Technology: A Strategic Plan for the Use of Advanced Technologies for Library Resource Sharing in New York State,* built around the following keystone goal:

> The *Library and Technology* plan must be viewed as the means by which any library—regardless of its size or location—enables its users to obtain access to information. All libraries in New York State—academic, school, public, and other—can become the Electronic Doorways through which *all* New Yorkers can reach the totality of information resources of the State. [Introduction 1]

As noted previously, in 1975, many rural community college librarians read similar words from the National Commission on Libraries and Information Science. Such a goal then seemed impossible. At that time, however, those librarians, frequently working in professional isolation, shared only a sense of impotence toward achieving excellence in their library services. Today, some of those librarians are providing access equal to that found in urban environments. They regularly experience the satisfying sense of empowerment that comes from competently utilizing computer technology to meet the growing demand for information from people who, like themselves, can now combine vocational achievement with the many benefits of rural living.

The infusion of technology and staff needed to equip rural community college libraries to meet their complex mission cannot be accomplished inexpensively. Annually, every community college develops its most important statement of philosophy and objectives. To learn what a college really stands for, don't just turn to its catalog, mission statement, or reports to accrediting agencies. Instead, examine closely its annual operating budget. Librarians must focus less on words and more on numbers. A critical measure of a library's success is whether financial resources are present in that annual budget that affirm the central role of the electronic library to the mission of the rural community college.

Even with strong college support, it will frequently be necessary for librarians to seek actively outside funding to accomplish their mission. This is a new but necessary role for community college library directors and staff. The librarian's most important task, however, is to demonstrate convincingly the importance of the new information resources to campus and community. Librarians must use the power of their initial electronic resources to garner support for further infusion of technology and staff into their new information centers.

In short, librarians must make the case. They must continually promote their vision of equal access to quality information services by demonstration of significant results for faculty, students, administrators, trustees, and community residents. The responsibility of rural community college administrators and community leaders is to be insightful enough to understand the opportunity before them, and wise enough to invest resources needed to enable their community college libraries to play a pivotal role in shaping an exciting future for rural America.

*   *   *

The author wishes to express his appreciation to the CCFL Division of Instructional Services staff members, who for ten years have invested so much time and energy in the goals described in this article; and to Dr. Charles J. Meder, President of the Community College of the Finger Lakes, who has supported the vision.

Works Consulted

Bell, Mary Beth, and Edwin Rivenburgh. "The Impact of Front-end Software on Search Training Programs in Small Academic Libraries." *Gateway Software and Natural Language Interfaces.* Ed. James A. Benson and Bella Hass Weinberg. Ann Arbor: Pierian Press, 1988. 40–48.

"Census Estimates Show Canandaigua Is Fastest Growing City in New York." (Canandaigua) *Daily Messenger* 11 Apr. 1989: A1.

Commission on the Future of Community Colleges. *Building Communities: A Vision for a New Century.* Washington, D.C.: American Association of Community and Junior Colleges, 1988.

Currin, Earl C., Jr., and W. Robert Sullins. "The Community College's Role in Rural Economic Development." *Community/Junior College Quarterly* 12 (1988): 37–46.

Eaton, John M. "Small Rural College: A Vital Component of the Delivery System." *Community and Junior College Journal* 52.2 (1981): 15–16.

Hacker, Andrew, ed. *U/S: A Statistical Portrait of the American People.* New York: Viking Press, 1983.

Johnson, Millard F., Jr. "After the Online Catalog: A Call for Active Librarianship." *American Libraries* 13 (1982): 235–239.

Ketchum, Richard M. "For Sale: Rural America." *Country Journal* May/June 1989: 80–83.

Long, Larry, and Diana DeAre. "The Slowing of Urbanization in the U.S." *Scientific American* 249.1 (1983): 33–41.

National Commission on Libraries and Information Science. *Toward a National Program for Library and Information Services: Goals for Action.* Washington: U.S. Government Printing Office, 1975.

New York State Library. Phase II Statewide Automation Committee. *Technology and Access: The Electronic Doorway Library.* Albany: University of the State of New York, State Education Department, New York State Library, Division of Library Development, 1989.

Vavrek, Bernard. "The Hidden Majority: Rediscovering Rural Libraries." *Wilson Library Bulletin* 58 (1983): 266–269.

"Yates County Losing Jobs; Ontario Gaining." (Canandaigua) *Daily Messenger* 12 Dec. 1989: A13.

TECHNICAL COLLEGE LIBRARIES: ON THE CUTTING EDGE

Judy Jorgensen and Ruth Ahl

"Library, library more than a book . . ." This old advertising jingle epitomizes life in a technical college library. Technical college libraries are different from community college libraries in their mission, their customers, and their services.

Waukesha County Technical College is a public postsecondary school which offers specific occupational training below the baccalaureate level. The setting is suburban, which makes WCTC unique among the 16 VTAE colleges in Wisconsin. The others are either urban or rural. WCTC's mission is formed in partnership with the community and the Wisconsin State Board of Vocational, Technical, and Adult Education. WCTC seeks to implement its philosophy by providing:

- Occupational competency programming, which offers the skills and knowledge required for entry-level positions, upgrading of existing skills, and training for occupational changes.
- Occupational upgrading and continuing-education offerings, which contribute to job-related lifelong learning.
- Basic-skills training needed to enter and succeed in occupational programs.
- Career planning opportunities, such as counseling, evaluation, and assessment.
- Economic development leadership through technical assistance, customized training, assessment of labor market/training needs, and identification of training needs required for emerging occupations.
- Career ladder opportunities, through cooperative relationships with area high schools and colleges, which seek to maximize students' educational endeavors.

- Personal-development-skills training, which improves an individual's ability to solve problems, cope with change, and adapt to new environments.
- Self-enrichment opportunities, which provide outlets for creative growth and expression.

The students who attend technical colleges, just like those who attend community colleges, are older (average age 27–29) than traditional 4-year-college students, are more likely to be from minority populations, and are enrolled for retraining or upgrading. They are most often part-time students, are employed either part-time or full-time, and have family responsibilities. These people come to the technical college with very definite goals and frequently have very tight time constraints to meet their goals. WCTC's students are here out of choice with clear occupational goals and a specific need for library information that is practical and technology based. This is a need that other area college and community libraries often cannot meet.

The college serves students, a few as young as 12 or 13, up to a large number of retirees. One of the dominant and often discussed characteristics of the students at the technical college is the wide diversity in both ability and previous academic experience. Because this is an open-entry institution, few programs require a high school diploma or GED. Admission into the college is open, although admission into specific programs may be restricted. Students range from those with very basic literacy skills to those with advanced degrees, including students with disabilities and limited English proficiency. WCTC has more advanced-degree students than any of the other 16 technical colleges in Wisconsin.

What effect does this heterogeneous student population have on the technical college library? First is the challenge of meeting the information needs of the different reading levels, print size, etc., within the highly varied occupational curricula. WCTC offers both associate degree and vocational diploma programs in a wide variety of occupations in service and health occupations, business, and industry. The next challenge is encouraging people to use the library who have little or no experience with a library. This is accomplished by tours, orientation sessions, advertisements in college publications, class visits, and through the location of the college learning center, The Learning Place, in the north end of the library. The Learning Place serves 1,500 to 2,000 students a year in tutorial and developmental activities and highly encourages the use of the library by these students. WCTC has a rather large group of both international students and educators whose English skills vary. This group poses yet another challenge to the library in finding technically appropriate materials for a limited-English-speaking population.

Customers of the college include not only students, but community members, and business and industry. In 1985 WCTC took a much more aggressive posture in serving the needs of business and industry. Courses had always been available to business and industry, but in 1985 the Business and Industry Services Division was established to market WCTC courses and programs actively to business and industry. This effort resulted in $1 million in contracts in 1989-90 and new demands on the college library by companies needing technical information, including information regarding the international market. The Waukesha County Board of Realtors is establishing and funding a collection within the WCTC library that will be available to both the real estate students and the 1,500 + real estate professionals in Waukesha County. The college and its library have become much more visible in the community and much more widely used.

The services of the WCTC library have become automated and computerized, allowing students and staff access to all library materials within the county and through WISPALS to two other Wisconsin technical colleges. The library has a large collection of handbooks, encyclopedias, dictionaries, and books on such topics as business, marketing, international trade, medicine, nursing, electronics, manufacturing, and the industrial trades.

Other resources are SIRS (Social Issues Resources Series—reprints of magazine and newspaper articles as well as government reports), SAMS Photofacts (Schematics), Company Annual Reports, InfoTrac (an automated references system that provides computer-aided retrieval of bibliographic references stored on compact discs), and Newsbank (newspaper articles from 130 U.S. papers on microfiche). There are approximately 36,000 books in the stacks and 440 current titles of magazines and newspapers in the collection.

The staff will search for books not on the shelf. Interlibrary loan service is available for items not in the WCTC collection. INFOPASS allows use of and sometimes checkout privileges in other libraries in the Milwaukee area. Other services include on-line data base searching of educational, business, scientific, and technical data bases; use of the photocopier and reader/printers; and checkout of audiocassette players.

Services extended to faculty include notification of newly acquired books, placement of items on reserve status, reservation of videotapes and films for classroom use, and library tours and orientation.

College librarians obtain their education in traditional academic settings. Most of them start working in community or traditional academic settings. For those who do work in technical college libraries the environment is stimulating. Most of the technical college libraries in Wisconsin have very small (one or two) professional staffs. They meet as a group frequently and call on each other for consultation and support.

The word that keeps surfacing during interviews is "variety." Because the professional staff is small, these librarians need to know budgeting, purchasing, and maintenance, as well as being subject-matter generalists and specialists. They need to be aware of the needs of local business: what they do and who their subsidiaries and suppliers are.

One of the pluses for technical college librarians is that customer service can be first. These professionals are, in most cases, not considered to be faculty but management, and so do not have the "publish or perish" encumbrances. The collections in these libraries are based more on current materials, especially periodicals, abstracts, and indices that are rarely kept over 10 years, and less on historical and research materials. The occupational curriculum changes constantly with new technologies and labor-market fluctuations. A heavy emphasis on periodicals allows the scope and emphasis of the library collection to change more rapidly.

Technical colleges are present, future, and change oriented. To be competitive and to serve the needs of the technical college faculty and students, they must be on the front line of technology. For the professional librarian who is challenged by constant change, technical college libraries are exciting environments.

The authors of this chapter interviewed technical college librarians throughout the United States. Five libraries of various size and geographical balance were questioned. Colleges in states with a number of technical school and colleges were selected. The individual responses showed some trends and innovative ideas designed to keep these libraries on the cutting edge of technology and of service to their clientele. Both written and telephone interviews were conducted.

Question 1: Where are you located on the college campus? Is this location a good one? If not, where would be a better location?

The responses ranged from the location being a showcase in a new building to being so far removed from the mainstream of college traffic that the library seemed to play a very secondary role within the college. The librarians interviewed believed that the classes, services, etc., that were close to the library were actually more important than the physical location. Because the traditional college research users of the library are not found at technical colleges and because often students have rarely used any library, being on a major traffic pattern at the college is essential.

Question 2: What is your college enrollment? What are the general demographics of the student population?

The technical colleges interviewed had full-time-equivalent (FTE) counts of between 1,050 and 18,000. The split between male and female was relatively equal, with females having a slightly higher percentage. This statistic would tend to correlate with the increasing number of women entering the work force. With one exception (a 50% non-white student base) each of the colleges had 22% or less minorities. However, the colleges believed these numbers to be steadily increasing. The average age of the students was 27.

Question 3: Is your library automated? What system or vendor? What functions?

Each of the colleges is automated; some are just beginning this process and others are well into the process.

Nashville State Technical Institute Library has been successfully using the SYRSI UNICORN System for their public access catalog and circulation for five years.

The Waukesha County Technical College Library along with Moraine Park Technical College and Gateway Technical College Libraries have recently formed the Wisconsin PALS Network (WISPALS) using the UNISYS PALS library system to automate library functions. The network will be open to other vocational technical libraries as well as other types of libraries within the state.

Some technical college libraries are using microcomputers for various library functions, including library literacy, as well as OCLC or Bibliofile for cataloging. Funding for library automation is sometimes the stumbling block, not a lack of desire on the part of the librarians to keep up with the technology. Some libraries are unable to afford OCLC for cataloging or DIALOG or BRS for data base searching. Compact disc technology may be the answer in the long term as costs come down.

Question 4: If your library is automated, what unique needs have you discovered for service that are peculiar to the two-year technical college? Please include things such as the impact of CDs on reference services to students, networking, and alternative delivery programs for library resources. *Is there interlinking cooperation between your college library and other area libraries (other schools, public and private libraries)?*

Technical college libraries are feeling the impact of technology on their services, particularly in the area of abstracts, indices, and other references that are now available on CDs such as *INFOTRAC–Magazine Index Plus, Grolier's Electronic Encyclopedia, ERIC (Educational Resources Information Center), NURSESEARCH–Nursing and Allied Health Index, Wilson-Disc (Readers' Guide to Periodical Literature, Business and Periodicals Index, Applied Science and Technology Index, etc.).* Alternative delivery programs are primarily done on cable TV to outreach campuses or centers. Librarians are finding it difficult to keep up with the demand for information at these sites. One innovative library director is faxing requested material to these outreach centers. Another college is offering the library as an alternative test-taking site.

Each library has an extensive network, some mainly within their communities and others statewide. Waukesha County Technical College in Wisconsin seems to have the widest interlinking network. The college belongs to the Waukesha

County Federated Library System, the Library Council of Metropolitan Milwaukee (this council includes public, private, school, and not-for-profit agency libraries), and the Wisconsin Inter-Library Services. The college also has access to WISCAT, the Wisconsin Catalog on Compact Disc, which allows searching for material statewide. There is also a van delivery service within the county among the 16 public libraries, WCTC, a private college (Carroll College), and the University of Wisconsin–Waukesha Center.

Question 5: How is your college library marketing itself to:

Faculty: One of the age-old problems in technical colleges is encouraging faculty use. A questionnaire administered to 138 full- and part-time vocational instructors at Tarrant County Junior College (Texas) showed that although printed materials were used in almost 75% of the courses, library-owned resources were used much less extensively than materials owned by the departments and instructors, even when the library holdings included the same books and periodicals. Teachers who were classified as library users believed that students should read more than textbook assignments and that library materials help keep students current in their field, and that library use develops critical thinking skills and improves grades. Non–library users indicated that they did not think that the library needed to be used in skill development courses and that library materials were not easily accessible to the classroom.

The question then becomes how to turn non-library-using faculty into library users. Very traditional means are being used: newsletters, orientations for new faculty, and an informal network. Albuquerque Technical Vocational Institute in New Mexico has an advisory committee made up of one representative from each instructional department on campus. This advisory committee meets two or three times a year to share information and need, and serves as the library link back to their departments. The colleges that reported having the library director at division chair or dean level seemed to think that the library marketing effort (newsletters, tours, and classes scheduled in the library) was easier due to the recognized status the library enjoyed.

Students: Again traditional methods of marketing to students are being used: articles in the student newspaper, classroom visits, tours, user guides distributed to all students. Nashville State Technical Institute in Tennessee sponsors a coffee break for evening-school students. This event gets them into the library.

Community: Marketing to the community appears to be lacking except at Nashville, where the building is new. Information reaches the community by word of mouth. Waukesha County Technical College has made it very easy for the public to return books by establishing a frontage-road book drop. Materials may also be returned at any of the county public libraries.

Question 6: Does your college have outreach to business and industry? If so, what has been the effect of this outreach on library resources?

The responses to this question ranged from little activity with no noticeable impact to Waukesha County Technical College's reporting that this was a major effort of the college and the one change that had a major impact on the request for library services. The need for the technical college library to be on the cutting edge of technology becomes even more critical if library services to business and industry are to be offered. Albuquerque Technical-Vocational Institute is providing bibliographies for micro-workshops for industry and would like to be able to do this for every class contracted by industry.

Question 7: Does your college have an academic support center on campus? If so, what has been the effect of this service on library resources? If applicable, please include any involvement with the literacy effort.

Each college interviewed has some sort of remedial or tutoring center located on the campus, although only two of the centers were tied in with the library: Albuquerque Technical-Vocational Institute and Waukesha County Technical College. Albuquerque has an Adult Learning Center that includes both student and professional tutors and literacy volunteers from both the student population and the community. Albuquerque has invested in video, software, and audio cassettes to assist the nonreader. WCTC's library houses a separate unit called The Learning Place, which is an adult individualized-learning center with remediation, pre-tech training, and tutorial support with a professional staff of 22.

The Learning Place also has extensive services for special-needs students, especially the learning disabled adult. The librarian at WCTC stated that, due to the proximity of The Learning Place, students are using the library who probably never would have. The library also purchases low-level reading material for the two outreach campuses with strong literacy programs.

Question 8: What are the top 2 to 4 issues facing your library today and in the future?

The issue that surfaced repeatedly is automation—"the need to bring us up to snuff," as one librarian stated. Linked to automation is networking. How can the library tie into other automated networks to give the student nearly unlimited access to information? The WISPALS consortium in Wisconsin is an example of this type of access. It is hoped that WISPALS as a consortium will access other networks and vice versa.

Another major concern is where library services are located within the organization and the role libraries are taking in a quickly changing technology. One librarian believes that a plan to separate library services into its own department with the director at dean level will increase the library's status and will allow it equal standing within the college, thus increasing usage. Another college states that retention is now the key, and more faculty are beginning to pay attention to the role the library might play in helping to retain students. A number of the technical colleges are expanding their mission and becoming more like community colleges. This switch in mission will undoubtedly have an effect on library use.

The last major issue that surfaced was the challenge to technical college libraries to assist students in understanding the uses of the library: the practical application of libraries. Technical college students are doers, not scholars, and it is part of the library's mission to encourage them to become lifelong library users. To meet this need, one of the colleges is collecting company annual reports and assisting students in using them. It certainly appears that technical colleges are on the brink of major changes in not only mission but also information-age, computer-based technologies.

Question 9: What is happening at your college or in your region that is interesting and innovative?

Each college had exciting new things to report:

Nashville State Technical Institute is emphasizing industry training and instrumentation, has a new service called the "Grammar Doctor" which allows anyone in the community to call in for help in grammar, and provides SI (supplemental instruction) for high-risk/high-failure-rate students by paying a successful student to retake a course and assist these students.

Waukesha County Technical College is heavily involved with business and industry outreach and contracted services, which are adding a new dimension to the demand for library services; it operates an International Trade Library (state's largest) as a part of the library. The available resources in the International Trade Library are both regional and topical and include books, periodicals, videotapes, and audiocassettes. The wide variety of information includes export assistance, marketing and distribution, transportation, banking, finance, and insurance language, travel guides and dictionaries, and cultural/business protocol.

Career Education, including career exploration, resume writing, interviewing, and career pathing is integral to WCTC's curriculum and services. The library has an extensive bibliography on career information that includes topics such as choosing a career, jobs of the future, changing careers, learning about technical and skilled jobs, short-term and part-time work, and small business careers. Career opportunities is such a hot topic that these materials have been arranged into a separate collection to serve both students and the local community better.

WCTC is involved in a consortium with two sister technical colleges to automate their libraries.

Albuquerque Technical-Vocational Institute is networking with the University of New Mexico for an academic data base that has outreach capabilities within a 30-mile radius and is planning a new campus within three years that will allow for a new library with automation and technology to meet the 21st century.

New Hampshire Technical Institute is also recognizing not only the technical changes in industry, but also the changes in the industries that are relocating to their area. The library is redirecting its resources to serve new customers.

Cincinnati Technical College reports that it is helping to fund a newspaper indexing project underway at the Public Library of Cincinnati and Hamilton County. Free dial access to this computer data base has been available since 1990. Searchers will be able to use keyboards and Boolean logic, and to limit searches by date and newspaper. Indexing for files from the Kenton County (Kentucky) Public Library and the Cincinnati Historical Society Library will be added at a later date.

Interviewing technical college librarians all across the country has been very enlightening. These colleges are preparing for the technological, mission, and student changes that are occurring and will continue to escalate through the 90's. Helping to keep the colleges and the students on the cutting edge is their goal and one they are determined to attain.

Acknowledgments

Sincere appreciation to the Library Directors:
Debbie Tucker, Reference Librarian, and James Horton, Director, from Cincinnati Technical College, Library, Cincinnati, Ohio
Carolyn Householder, Educational Resource Center, Nashville State Technical Institute, Nashville, Tennessee
Charles Baldonado, Library Services, Albuquerque Technical-Vocational Institute, Albuquerque, New Mexico
John Hane, Farnum Library, New Hampshire Technical Institute, Concord, New Hampshire
Marion Vogel, Palmer Campus Learning Resources Center, Trident Technical College, Charleston, South Carolina

Bibliography

Lolley, John L., "Vocational Teachers and the College Library"; Research report, Tarrant County Junior College, Texas. 1980.
McCarthy, Robert, "The New Library/Media Center"; *Electronic Learning*. May/June 1990, pp. 25–28.
Reinhard, Bill, "South Carolina's Technical Colleges Become Comprehensive"; *Community, Technical, and Junior College Times*. Vol. 1, #23. November 21, 1989.

Woodsworth, Anne, "The Impact of Globalizing a Campus Library"; *Cause/Effect*. Summer 1989, pp. 3–5.

"Savannah Tech on the Cutting Edge of Library Technology"; *AACJC Journal*. October/November 1989, p. 80.

"South Carolina Developing Statewide Network"; *Wilson Library Bulletin*. June 1986, p. 13.

LIBRARY RESOURCE CENTRES IN CANADA

Alan Dyment

Canada's colleges and provincial college systems are characterized as much by their differences as by their similarities,
and it would certainly be inaccurate to refer to a Canadian
public college "system." In each province, special circumstances sparked the establishment of new colleges, and even
though they all came into being within the same short time
span, they were meant to serve different social purposes, to
have different priorities, and to operate on a day-to-day basis
in quite different ways. The last ten years have seen these
differences accentuated as they grew beyond infancy and
settled into serving longer-term objectives.[1]

Canadian community colleges and institutes of technology
are noted for their diversity in almost all aspects of their
operation, including role, student population, administrative
structure, and curriculum. Community colleges in Canada
have a relatively short history and have developed in different
ways. In Ontario, for instance, twenty community colleges
were established within a three-year period so that:

> By January 1971, there were over 30,000 full-time
> post-secondary students enrolled in programs in some
> seventy significant locations as well as such unique
> "campuses" as two trap-lines in the northern bush, a
> trailer parked where required in the inner core of
> Toronto, and a bus exploring eastern Canada.[2]

The experiences recorded by three librarians in the early
days of the Ontario college system are typical of those in
other Canadian colleges at that time:

> On opening day 1967 the library resources of Niagara
> College consisted of a room (a double classroom with a

small office), some furniture and shelves, two and a half staff (the other half taught the library technician program), and no books or other library material.[3]

A library at Loyalist got off to a rather slow start in August 1967. There was one librarian and no material in space shared with the secondary school in which the college was housed. The workroom cum office had to accommodate two librarians—the college's and the school's—plus clerical staff.[4]

The library was located in a kindergarten room in the old James S. Bell public school and the equipment at that time consisted of a librarian's desk and a pair of scissors purchased from Woolworth's.[5]

In Canada it is the provincial governments which have the responsibility for provision of educational services. The role played by provincial governments in the administration of colleges may be direct (as in Manitoba and New Brunswick), coordinating (as in Quebec and Nova Scotia), or indirect (as in Alberta), but has been strengthened in the 1980s as governments have responded to demand for greater fiscal restraint and accountability. At the same time, new or expanded systems of community colleges are emerging in Nova Scotia, Newfoundland, Saskatchewan, and in the Yukon and Northwest Territories. As a consequence of austerity measures imposed by provincial governments, growth of existing library and learning resource services came to a standstill or even regressed in such provinces as Quebec and British Columbia, while new services and facilities are opening elsewhere, albeit with modest resources. Even the fundamental nature of two-year institutions has been challenged by the announcement of degree-granting status to three community colleges in British Columbia.

Changes in the student populations, the impact of new technologies, political and socioeconomic pressures, and increased demand for accountability have combined to transform the environment in which Canadian community colleges, institutes of technology, and their library resource services operate. There are no national research or statistical data related to library resource centres in Canadian two-year post-secondary institutions; even Statistics Canada no longer publishes community college library statistics. There are also very few publications dealing with libraries and learning resource centres in Canadian community colleges and institutes of technology, with much of the material being elusive and ephemeral.

In 1988-89, this writer undertook a study which examined the organizational structures, administration, and services of libraries and learning resource centres (library resource centres, or LRCs) in Canadian community colleges and institutes of technology, and identified current issues and concerns. The scope of the study was limited to library resource centres in Canadian publicly funded community colleges and institutes of technology. The latter was established to meet province-wide needs for technical programs, but the distinctions between community colleges and institutes of technology have become increasingly blurred. The study included the Collèges d'Enseignement Général et Professionnel (CEGEPs) of Quebec, but excluded private colleges, vocational centres, single-purpose or highly specialized colleges, and all degree-granting institutions.

The total number of Canadian colleges and institutes of technology for the purposes of the study was found to be 129, of which 118 were community colleges and 11 were institutes of technology. A survey questionnaire was mailed to all of the library resource centres, and a final response rate of 77% was obtained. The survey data were supplemented by information and opinions gathered from a series of directed interviews with twenty-three principal administrators of library resource centres in selected community colleges and institutes of technology across the country. Colleges and institutes from all ten provinces and the Yukon Territory are represented in the data. Distribution of the institutions by student full-time-equivalent enrolment (FTE) was: under 1,000 FTE—20%; 1,000–1,999 FTE—22%; 2,000–2,999 FTE—16%; 3,000–3,999 FTE—19%; 4,000–4,999 FTE—7%; 5,000 FTE and over—15%.

Reporting Relationships and Position Titles of LRC Principal Administrators

Of the LRC principal administrators, 22% report directly to a dean; an additional 21% report to an academic director, while 11% report to an academic vice-president. The data show a great diversity of reporting relationships for LRC principal administrators, but only 13% of library resource centres are clearly located in a non-academic division. An increasing number are reporting to administrators with responsibility for a range of academic and student support services, rather than to those having direct responsibility for the instructional program. Multi-campus institutions are administered with diverse organizational structures, but there are only five community colleges which maintain autonomous library resource centres on separate campuses.

More than fifty different position titles for LRC principal administrators were reported, with 20% categorized as "Director," 15% "Coordinator," 14% "Manager," and 14% as "Librarian." Of the English-language position titles, 43% include expressions such as "Learning Resources" or "Resource Centre," while 35% incorporate the words "Library" or "Librarian."

LRC Organizational Structures and Administration

Of the thirty-eight organization charts submitted by survey respondents, 71% use function as the primary basis for organization, while 26% use geographical location as the primary factor in determining organizational structure, usually using function at a secondary level, particularly for technical services and audiovisual equipment services. In response to a question about organizational change, half of the respondents reported that such change had occurred in the LRC within the past five years, and 31% indicated that changes are planned within the next two years.

The average number of librarians employed in LRCs is 1.7 FTE (full-time equivalent), in addition to the principal administrator (who may not always be a professional librarian).

More than 71% of all LRCs serving enrolments of fewer than 2,000 FTE students have no professional librarian other than the LRC principal administrator. Canadian LRCs employ an average of 4.6 FTE technical and clerical support staff for each professional librarian. Library technicians are employed in a variety of capacities in Canadian LRCs, and often undertake responsibilities which would be considered within the realm of professional librarians in other academic library settings; 83% of respondents reported that non-professional staff routinely respond to reference questions that require the use of reference tools.

Excluding the principal administrator, 51% of librarians receive full faculty status, and a further 15% have partial faculty status. The rationale for faculty status of librarians employed in Canadian community colleges and technical institutes has been presented in *Guidelines for Academic Status for Professional Librarians in Community and Technical Colleges.*[6] The majority of administrators interviewed favored faculty status for librarians, and no longer consider it to be a major issue. In Quebec, where librarians and spécialistes en moyen et techniques d'enseignement (SMTE) are classified as members of a professional staff group but lack faculty status, LRC administrators held the view that this group enjoyed one of the best contracts available to CEGEP personnel.

The survey showed that 55% of responding LRCs have formal programs for evaluation of professional personnel, although significantly fewer LRCs in Quebec maintain such programs; 58% of LRCs reported participation in formal planning processes; and 49% maintained formal mission statements. An increasing number of Canadian colleges and institutes of technology are now engaging in institutional strategic planning processes as they evolve from developmental stages to organizational maturity.

Budgets and Financial Resources

The survey data reveal a mean LRC operating budget of $600,830, with a range between $46,127 and $2,553,025. The mean percentage of institutional operating budgets allocated to library resource centres is 2.9%, representing an

average LRC operating budget of $221 per FTE student, and
an average acquisitions budget of $39 per FTE student. The
data indicate considerable variations in levels of operating and
acquisitions budgets per student between provinces, and also
between community colleges and institutes of technology,
with the latter generally receiving higher levels of LRC funding than community colleges. Fifteen respondents reported
participation in fund-raising activities to supplement budget
allocations, although revenues are modest. The two-year institution in Canada has suffered from a lack of well-
established alumni associations, but as colleges and institutes
approach significant anniversaries of their founding, there is a
growing interest in the establishment of such bodies.

Services

The primary factor in considering access to services is the
number of hours of service provided by the library resource
centre during a regular semester period. Among the Canadian
community colleges and institutes of technology responding
to the survey questionnaire, the mean weekly semester hours
of service was 62.3 hours per week, with a range from 21 to
85 hours per week.

The table below summarizes the student, faculty, and institutional services offered by at least 10% of the survey respondents:

Service	Percentage
Library instruction for classes	95%
Audiovisual equipment in the LRC	88
Student guide to the LRC	88
Faculty guide to the LRC	77
Distribution of audiovisual equipment	71
On-line search services for faculty	64
Maintenance of audiovisual equipment	59
On-line search services for students	48
Audiovisual production services	46
Microcomputers in the LRC	44
Inventory of microcomputer software	44
Audiovisual guide to the LRC	34

Service	Percentage
College archives	33
Instructional design support services	30
Microcomputers outside the LRC	14
Distribution of instructional computing equipment	13
Maintenance of instructional computing equipment	11
Computer managed learning/instruction design & production	11

Fewer than half of Canadian college and institute LRCs provide such services as on-line searches for students, audiovisual production, access to microcomputers and software, and instructional design support. Fewer than 15% have responsibility for microcomputer services other than those within the LRC, instructional computing equipment distribution or maintenance, CML/CAI design and production support, printing and graphic services, or remedial/developmental services. There is a much greater emphasis placed upon library and audiovisual resources and services than on those other instructional components of a comprehensive learning resources program as envisaged in much of the literature of the 1970s.

Only 20% of responding library resource centres have formal programs for the evaluation of their services. Institutional evaluations, such as those which all community colleges in British Columbia are required to undergo every five years, may provide an intensive but infrequent evaluation exercise. Changes in administrative leadership may also stimulate evaluation. Much of the recent literature on excellence reinforces the need for ongoing evaluation, particularly of client services; it is to be hoped that more Canadian library resource centres will become engaged in evaluation activities in the future.

Technical Services, Circulation Systems, and Automation

The Library of Congress classification system is used by 61% of responding LRCs, and 39% use the Dewey decimal system; in institutes of technology, the Dewey decimal system predominates. Further, 54% of LRCs still maintain card catalogues, 38% use microfiche, 23% provide on-line public access catalogues, and 12% use computer printouts for public access to their collections; 27% of respondents are using more than one type of catalogue format. Use of a card catalogue predominates in those institutions with fewer than 3,000 FTE students, while card catalogues are found in only a minority of LRCs in institutions with enrolments exceeding 3,000 FTE.

Of responding LRCs, 61% are participating in a computerized network for cataloguing data. If the data are analyzed by category of institution, only 18% of LRCs in institutes of technology participate in computerized networks. This difference between library resource centres in colleges and those in technical institutes is accentuated because of the involvement of community colleges in Ontario and Quebec in provincial networks; there are no institutes of technology in those provinces. The Ontario College Bibliocentre provides a centralized acquisition, cataloguing, and processing service for all of the province's community colleges. In Quebec, thirty-six French-language CEGEPs are participating in RENARD (Réseau Normalisé et Automatisé des Ressources Documentaires)—a network intended to support acquisitions, cataloguing, electronic mail, interlibrary loan, reference, and, at a local level, circulation. There is no national cooperative network operating in Canada.

CD-ROM is being used for cataloguing support by 22% of responding LRCs, primarily in British Columbia and Alberta—provinces which do not have formal provincial networks. On-line acquisition systems are in place in 54% of the responding LRCs, and 64% have automated at least a portion of their acquisitions processes. The use of manual systems predominates, however, in LRCs serving fewer than 3,000 FTE students.

Manual circulation procedures are used by 70% of responding LRCs. On-line systems exceed manual systems only in those institutions with enrolments of more than 5,000 FTE students. The majority of on-line systems in use are software packages purchased from vendors and operating on a variety of hardware configurations from microcomputers to mainframes. Fully integrated circulation/acquisition/cataloguing systems are in use by 17% of responding LRCs. Only one of these fully integrated systems has been developed in-house. Many LRC administrators have completed extensive reviews of available integrated systems, and are developing proposals or are awaiting funding decisions. It is probable that a further survey in five years' time would reveal major changes in the numbers of Canadian LRCs with integrated systems.

Collections

The average number of volumes per FTE student in Canadian library resource centres is 23.5, with collection size ranging from under 10,000 to over 130,000 print volumes. The average number of periodical titles is 547. Average audiovisual holdings include 527 16mm films and 1,271 video recordings. Forty-three percent of responding LRCs include microcomputer software in their collections, with a range of holdings between 10 and 2,564 items; 36% of LRCs report intershelving of at least part of their audiovisual holdings with their print collection, but only 5% provide complete physical integration.

Selection of materials for the majority of LRC collections is considered to be a responsibility shared equally by LRC personnel and instructional staff; 35% of respondents stated that LRC staff were primarily responsible for selection, while 8% reported that this responsibility rested primarily with the teaching faculty.

When the majority of Canadian community colleges were being established, it was extremely difficult to obtain resource materials that were appropriate for the needs of their students and faculty. The majority of materials had been written or produced for either school-age or university-level students; even when the market had grown, problems of obtaining appropriate resource materials continued, particularly in the technical area of curricula. Canadian LRCs were also facing increasing pressure for materials written and produced in Canada and presenting a Canadian perspective.

While many LRCs continue to struggle to locate appropriate material for students with low literacy levels, others are facing the challenge to expand their collections to accommodate the requirements of third- and fourth-year university level programs. Colleges in British Columbia, Alberta, and Quebec, for example, offer university-transfer programs, while those in Ontario, Manitoba, and New Brunswick do not. As more colleges become involved with offering higher level university courses and, in consequence, hire instructors with post-graduate degrees, demands of faculty members for research materials will increase.

The existence of a multi-campus environment has a significant impact upon the LRC collection. The survey reported that 53% of respondents maintain staffed library resource centres on other campuses. In Canada, campuses of a single college may be hundreds of miles apart, rather than being in different districts of the same city.

Canadian Standards and Guidelines

In 1972, at the time when Canadian community college library standards were being developed, Murray observed:

> Library standards reflect the objectives and priorities of the nation that produces them, and change as the nation changes. Canadian standards show evidence of the shifting relationships between the federal, provincial, and local governments, the leadership newly assumed by the federal government in the provision of information to citizens, the effects of urbanization, a developing consciousness of social responsibility, and, above all, the rapidly changing patterns of education.[7]

One of these "rapidly changing patterns of education" was the Canadian community college, where enrolments had risen by 75% between 1967-68 and 1971-72. In 1973 the first and only national set of standards for library resource centres in Canadian community colleges and institutes of technology was published.[8]

The Canadian *Standards* contain both quantitative and qualitative standards. A common criticism of the document is that the quantitative standards are unrealistically high. The *Standards* were developed at a time when community colleges were developing at a rapid pace, and when financial constraint was not the pressing issue that it has become in the past decade. Twenty-five years ago, the authors believed the *Standards* to be optimistic but achievable. The Canadian *Standards* can also be faulted for their generality, particularly in terms of qualitative statements. Despite the legitimate concerns and criticisms that can be expressed about their usefulness today, many community college librarians have found the *Standards* to be helpful, particularly in the developmental years of library resource centres in Canada. Until 1990, attempts to update the Canadian *Standards* had been unsuccessful, despite the fact that they do not address current issues such as the pervasive applications of information technology, the expanding roles of library resource centres, the growth of computer software as a resource, changing methods of program delivery, etc. Increasingly, Canadian college librarians are referring to U.S. standards rather than to Canadian sources, and a Canadian version of U.S. documentation is under consideration by the Community and Technical College Libraries Section (CTCL) of the Canadian Association of College and University Libraries (CACUL).

Provincially, standards and guidelines have been produced in British Columbia, Alberta, and Quebec. Extensive work in British Columbia led to the development in 1981 of "management indicators" in the areas of collections, staff, and facilities, identified in grids which incorporated three major variables: geographical area, size of institution, and type of student user group.[9] The proposed management indicators were never adopted in British Columbia, and their structure precluded application for colleges outside the province.

In 1977 the Alberta Council of College Librarians (ACCL) produced a draft document recommending standards applicable to LRCs in public colleges, institutes of technology, and vocational centres in Alberta.[10] It was unusual in that separate modules were developed for each of the three major categories of non-degree-granting institutions in the province. The draft document was used informally by many Alberta college librarians, but it was never formally adopted, ACCL preferring to endorse the 1973 Canadian *Standards.*

In 1974, the Commission des Coordonnateurs de Bibliothèque of the Quebec Fédération des Cégeps published library standards for the Quebec colleges.[11] The *Normes* included guidelines regarding roles, organizational structure, staffing, collection size, budget, and facilities. In 1975, a second document was issued[12] which presented quantitative recommendations regarding staffing levels, organizational structures, print and audiovisual collections, and budgets for LRCs serving enrolments of two thousand and four thousand students.

In Nova Scotia, the Working Committee on Library/ Resource Centres has recently issued its report,[13] which outlines requirements for the development of library resource centres in the newly established Nova Scotia Community College system. The report provides draft qualitative and quantitative standards and guidelines in the areas of personnel, facilities, administration, budget, collections, and services. No other provinces have developed LRC standards or guidelines, although some provincial governments, such as Ontario, developed formulae for specific aspects of library resource services as part of their overall planning processes for college development.

Issues and Challenges for Canadian LRCs

Major issues identified by at least 10% of the responding LRCs include: automation (42%), budget and resources (34%), staffing levels (26%), acquisitions and collections (24%), space and facilities (20%), and impact of new technology (11%). In reply to a question which asked for identification of the most serious weaknesses of their library resource centres, the following were mentioned by at least 10% of the respondents: inadequate staffing levels (42%), inadequate collections or acquisitions (39%), inadequate facilities (35%), and inadequate level of automation (25%). New initiatives planned by at least 10% of the respondents for implementation in the coming two years were: automation projects (74%), planning new or renovated facilities (22%), installation of CD-ROM equipment (13%).

LRC principal administrators were also asked in directed interviews to identify issues which they consider to be of major significance for Canadian library resource centres in the coming five years. Issues identified included: resource sharing, cooperation and networking, interconnection of systems (27%); changes in curriculum and program delivery, including distance education (27%); articulation of role and value of LRC services; public relations (27%); changes in nature of student body, including mature and part-time students (23%); new technologies and their effect on the library resource centre (23%); fiscal restraint (18%); becoming more politically astute, e.g., negotiating skills, communication (14%); student literacy levels (14%); and degree-granting status (14%).

The issues identified above, with the exception of degree-granting status, are probably a reasonable indication of those which are uppermost in the minds of LRC administrators across Canada in 1990.

Canadian library resource centres are generally under-resourced for the tasks they should fulfil; this is particularly true of small colleges with only one professional librarian and limited staff support in the LRC. Only 18% of responding LRCs met the minimum U.S. "quantitative standards"[14] in four critical categories: number of librarians; number of clerical and technical support staff; size of collection; and number of periodical titles. Library resource centres in British Columbia have been the most successful in meeting quantitative standards, followed by Alberta, Ontario, and Quebec. It is worthy of note that these are the provinces which have also undertaken a considerable number of cooperative ventures.

Challenges for Canadian library resource centres in the coming decade will be many and varied. In British Columbia, the decision to give degree-granting status to three community colleges is having a great impact on the LRCs in those institutions. In Alberta, approval has been given for several colleges to increase the range of university-transfer programming, and it is possible that degree-granting status could follow for some institutions. The establishment in 1988 of the Saskatchewan Institute of Applied Science and Technology, and of the Nova Scotia Community College, heralded fundamental changes in institutional roles for these two provinces, with new opportunities for LRC administrators to develop cooperative structures leading to integrated library resource centres. New LRCs have been opened in New Brunswick, and working committees have been established to recommend standards and a common automated library system for all campus LRCs. In Newfoundland, the three institutes of technology are amalgamating with the province's five community colleges. The Atlantic Provinces Library Association has established a new interest group for community and technical college librarians, presenting new opportunities to improve the inadequate resources in those provinces. It is possible that Ontario might consider the introduction of university-transfer programs in some of its community colleges, although at present the clear distinctions between the two categories of post-secondary education in that province remain. Colleges in Quebec still face restraint in the future as their student population, predominantly of seventeen- to twenty-one-year-olds, declines, and there are no indications of expansion in Manitoba. In contrast, new library resource centre construction is occurring in British Columbia, Alberta, and Ontario, and there are indications that some regional colleges in Saskatchewan will be establishing library services for the first time.

Cooperative measures undertaken by library resource centres in western Canada continue to offset the effects of fiscal restraint. Current joint initiatives in British Columbia, coordinated by the Council of Post-Secondary Library Directors, include investigation of a province-wide on-line data base of film and video holdings to supplement BC-Net, a provincial interlibrary loan consortium which includes the university libraries. Another consortium of British Columbia LRCs with common mainframe computer systems has completed installation of automated cataloguing and circulation systems at relatively low cost. Three college LRCs in Alberta cooperated in 1988 to obtain favorable terms from a vendor for installation of integrated library systems. The Alberta Association of College Librarians has commissioned a video program on behalf of its member colleges, and has formed a program committee to arrange travelling workshops in order to support personnel with limited resources for professional development and travel.

Throughout this chapter, the diversity of library resource centres and their parent institutions has been stressed, and

Dennison and Gallagher forecast continued diversity among Canadian community colleges and institutes of technology in the future:

> Each college or college system must set its own future in consideration of its history, current realities, and the needs of the population to be served in different parts of the country. . . . There is no universally suitable choice of action, just as there is no ideal college model for Canada. All the issues call for fresh vision, anticipation and change. Canada's colleges have the people to reassess, to anticipate, and to map better futures.[15]

Endnotes

1. John D. Dennison and Paul Gallagher, *Canada's Community Colleges: A Critical Analysis* (Vancouver: University of British Columbia Press, 1986), p. 133.
2. Ontario. Department of Education. School Planning and Building Research, *The College Resource Centre: Colleges of Applied Arts and Technology* (Toronto: Department of Education, 1971), p. 11.
3. Stephen J. Kees, "Niagara College Resource Services," *COM-O-LIB,* 6 (August 1977), 51.
4. "Anderson Resource Centre—Loyalist College," *COM-O-LIB,* 6 (August 1977), 43.
5. A. MacLellan, "Humber College Learning Resource Centre (Née Libraries)," *COM-O-LIB,* 6 (August 1977), 34.
6. Canadian Association of College and University Libraries. Community and Technical College Libraries Section, *Guidelines for Professional Librarians in Community and Technical Colleges* (Ottawa: Canadian Library Association, 1978).
7. Florence B. Murray, "Canadian Library Standards," *Library Trends,* 21 (October 1972), 298.
8. Canadian Association of College and University Libraries, *Standards Recommended for Canadian Community College Libraries* (Ottawa: Canadian Library Association, 1973).
9. Ron J. Welwood, "Management Indicators for B.C. Learning Resource Centres," *Canadian Library Journal,* 39 (June 1982), 165–70.
10. Alberta Council of College Librarians, "Standards for Learning Resource Services, Preliminary Draft" (n.p., 1977).

11. Fédération des Cégeps. Commission des Coordonnateurs de Bibliothèque, *Normes des Bibliothèques de Cégep* (Montreal: Fédération des Cégeps, 1974).
12. Fédération des Cégeps. Commission des Directeurs de Bibliothèque, *Normes des Bibliothèques de Cégep, Doc. no. 2: Quantification* (Montreal: Fédération des Cégeps, 1975).
13. "Learning Resource Centres and Career Information in the Nova Scotia Community College System: Report of the Working Committee on Library/Resource Centres, January 1989" (n.p., 1989).
14. Association of College and Research Libraries. Ad Hoc Subcommittee to Develop Quantitative Standards for the "Guidelines for Two-Year College Learning Resources Programs," "Draft: Statement on Quantitative Standards for Two-Year Learning Resources Programs," *College and Research Libraries News,* 40 (March 1979), 69–73.
15. Dennison and Gallagher, *Canada's Community Colleges,* p. 140.

Selected Bibliography

Alberta Council of College Librarians. "Standards for Learning Resource Services: Preliminary Draft." N.p., 1977.

Allard, C. Gabriel. *Programme pour la Construction d'une Bibliothèque au Collège d'Enseignement Général et Professionnel de Maisonneuve.* Montreal: Bibliothèque du Collège de Maisonneuve, 1971.

"Anderson Resource Centre—Loyalist College," *COM-O-LIB,* 6 (August 1977), 43–50.

Baillargeon, Danièle, and Dufort, Robert. "Les Bibliothèques de Collège Confrontées au Problème des Non-Usagers," *Documentation et Bibliothéques,* 28 (October–December 1982), 155–60.

"Bibliothèque du Collège de Saint-Laurent," *Architecture Concept,* 28 (January–February 1973), 17–19.

British Columbia Library Association. "British Columbia College and Institute Library Brief," *BCLA Reporter,* 29 (July 1985), 13–16.

CAAT Tracks: Newsletter of the Committee on Learning Resources, Ontario Colleges of Applied Arts and Technology. N.p.: Committee on Learning Resources, Ontario Colleges of Applied Arts and Technology, 1986–.

Canada. Dominion Bureau of Statistics. *Survey of Libraries /Relevé des Bibliothèques, Part II: Academic Libraries /Bibliothèques Scolaires.* Ottawa: Queen's Printer, 1958–70.

Canada. Statistics Canada. *University and College Libraries in Canada /Bibliothèques des Universités et des Collèges du Canada.* Ottawa: Statistics Canada, 1972–81.

Canadian Association of College and University Libraries. *Standards Recommended for Canadian Community College Libraries.* Ottawa: Canadian Library Association, 1973.

Canadian Association of College and University Libraries. Community and Technical College Libraries Section. *Canadian Community and Technical College Libraries Directory, 1987.* Ottawa: Canadian Library Association, 1987.

————. *Directory of Community and Technical College Libraries and Resource Centres in Canada.* Ottawa: CTCL, 1980.

————. *Guidelines for Academic Status for Professional Librarians in Community and Technical Colleges.* Ottawa: Canadian Library Association, 1978.

Carpenter, Doreen. "History of the Bibliocentre," *COM-O-LIB,* 8 (September 1980), 22–25.

Carter, Ross. "The B.C. College Library Collections Development Project: Report on Phase One," *BCLA Reporter,* 21 (January–February 1978), 4–6.

————. "College and Institute Libraries: A Status Report," *BCLA Reporter,* 29 (March 1985), 5–7.

————. "Community College Library Service in British Columbia," *British Columbia Library Quarterly,* 37 (Spring 1974), 4–17.

Christensen, Philip. "St. Lawrence Learning Centre: A Model for the Future," *Media Message,* 7 (Fall 1977), 8–10.

COM-O-LIB: Newsletter of the Community College Librarians in Ontario. N.p.: Committee of Librarians of the Colleges of Applied Arts and Technology in Ontario, 1971–85.

Committee of Librarians of the Colleges of Applied Arts and Technology in Ontario. "Role Statements for Ontario CAAT Learning Resource Centres." N.p., 1984.

Council of Post-Secondary Library Directors. "Learning Resource Centres Roles Statement." N.p., 1978.

CTCL Communiqué. N.p.: CTCL, 1980–.

CTCL Newsletter. N.p.: CTCL, 1978–80.

Dakshinamurti, Ganga; Hunter, Ken; Bozyk, Patricia; and Saull, Ron. "An On-Line Library System, an 'In House' Development." Winnipeg, Man.: N.p., n.d.

Davidson-Arnott, Frances, comp. *Policies and Guidelines Developed for Community and Technical College Libraries.* Ottawa: Canadian Library Association, 1983.

Davidson-Arnott, Frances, and Dempster, Dora. "Report to CTCL and CLR on Standards," *CTCL Communiqué,* Fall/Winter 1986, pp. 5–7.

Di Liamchin, Lana, ed. *Director of Community and Technical College Libraries, Resource and Media Centres in Canada.* St. Anne-de-Bellevue, Que.: John Abbott College, 1975.

Downs, Judy. "The Role of the Librarian in the Curriculum Process Through Involvement in the Formal Committee Structure," *COM-O-LIB,* 13 (December 1985), 26–30.

Dube, Gilles. "Au Cégep de Rivière-du-Loup: Une Nouvelle Bibliothèque," *Argus,* 5 (January–February 1976), 7–9.

Dyment, Alan. *Library Resource Centres in Canadian Community Colleges and Institutes of Technology: Organizational Structures, Administration and Services—Summary of Data.* Ottawa: Canadian Association of College and University Libraries, 1991.

Edelman, Maria. "Survey of Small Libraries," *COM-O-LIB,* 9 (September 1981), 8–16.

Epp, Mary Anne. "Serving Print-Impaired Students at British Columbia Community College Libraries," *PNLA Quarterly,* 49 (Winter 1985), 3–4, 13

Fédération des Cégeps. Commission des Coordonnateurs de Bibliothèque. *Normes des Bibliothèques de Cégep.* Montreal: Fédération des Cégeps, 1974.

Fédération des Cégeps. Commission des Directeurs de Bibliothèque. *Normes des Bibliothèques de Cégep, Doc. no. 2: Quanitification.* Montreal: Fédération des Cégeps, 1975.

Feeley, James. "The CAAT's Meow: Libraries in Ontario Community Colleges," *Ontario Library Review* 61 (September 1977), 184–94.

Fraser, Barbara Mackay. "The Development of a Library Instruction Programme: A Case Study of a Large Canadian Community College." M. Lib. thesis, College of Librarianship, Aberystwyth, Wales, 1988.

Goldstein, S. "Introducing the Community College Library," *Ontario Library Review,* 53 (March 1969), 24–26.

Hanafi, Betty. "College's LRC Is More Than a Library," *BCLA Reporter,* 22 (August–September 1978), 6–7.

Hanafi, W. E., and Husband, B. E. "Report of the British Columbia College and Institute Learning Resources Centre Standards Project, Phase 1." N.p., 1979.

Harvey, Serge, and Maltais, Jacques. "Si RENARD, M'Était Conté:

Un Réseau Original pour les Collèges du Québec," *Argus,* 15 (June 1986), 49–57.

Howell, R. "Mount Royal, Where Islands Move the Media," *Canadian University and College,* 8 (March–April 1973), 33–34.

Hull, Philip. "The Learning Resource Centre at Georgian College: A Review and Future Directions—A Manager's View," *COM-O-LIB,* 9 (March 1981), 71–72.

Kees, Stephen J. "Niagara College Resource Services," *COM-O-LIB,* 6 (August 1977), 51–54.

Lajeunesse, Marcel, and Morin, Daniel. "Les Bibliothèques des Collèges d'Enseignement Général et Professionnel du Québec (1969–1983): Services Pédagogiques ou Comptoirs de Prêt?" *Argus,* 15 (June 1986), 33–47.

Le, Vinh. "Required Reading Database for the Health Sciences Programs at Seneca College Leslie Campus Resource Centre," *CAAT Tracks,* 1 (September 1986), 21–27.

"Learning Resource Centres and Career Information in the Nova Scotia Community College System: Report of the Working Committee on Library/Resource Centres, January 1989." N.p., 1989.

Lemaire, Jean. "L'Apprentissage du Travail Personnel et de l'Utilisation de la Bibliothèque au dans les Cégeps du Québec," *Argus,* 7 (March–April 1978), 38–43.

Léveillé, Jean M. Bernard. "L'Evolution de la Coopération dans les Bibliothèques de Collège du Québec," *Documentation et Bibliothèques,* 23 (September 1977), 135–41.

———. *Programme pour la Construction d'une Bibliothèque au CEGEP de Saint-Laurent.* Travaux et Documents, no. 4. Montreal: Association Canadienne des Bibliothécaires de Langue Française, 1971.

Lloyd, Patricia. "Survey of Evaluation Techniques Used for Librarians in English-Speaking Canadian Community College Libraries." N.p., n.d.

MacLellan, A. "Humber College Learning Resource Centre (Née Libraries)," *COM-O-LIB,* 6 (August 1977), 34–39.

Macmillian, Marionne. "Langara Library Overhauls Orientation Programme," *BCLA Reporter,* 21 (September–October 1977), 7–8.

Mansbridge, John. "Evaluating Resource Sharing Library Networks." Ph.D. dissertation, Case Western Reserve University, 1984.

Murphy, Angèle. "Les Normes des Bibliothèques de Collège: Le Québec Rattrapera-t-il le Pas?" *Documentation et Bibliothèques,* 19 (December 1973), 161–64.

North, John. "Towards Decentralization: The Learning Resource

Centre of Mount Royal College," *Canadian Library Journal,* 30 (May–June 1973), 236–42.

North, John, and Bishop, Elizabeth. "DOBIS/LIBIS: Online Circulation Control at Ryerson," *Library Journal,* 108 (June 15, 1983), 1221–25.

Ontario. Department of Education. Information Branch. *Basic Documents: Colleges of Applied Arts and Technology.* 3d printing with revisions. Toronto: Department of Education, 1967.

Ontario. Department of Education. School Planning and Building Research. *The College Resource Centre: Colleges of Applied Arts and Technology.* Toronto: Department of Education, 1971.

Prokopec, Douglas. "The Learning Resources Centre in the Canadian Community College," *Media Message,* 5 (Spring 1976), 7–12.

Québec (Province). Ministère de l'Education. Direction Générale de l'Enseignement Collégial. *Guide Pratique pour la Construction et l'Aménagement d'une Bibliothèque de CEGEP.* Québec: Ministère de l'Education, 1968.

Rolland, Joanne, "A Look at Ontario LRCs," *Canadian Library Journal,* 40 (June 1983), 157–61.

Stilborn, Linda. "A Comparative Look at Ontario Community College Resource Centres," *COM-O-LIB,* 13 (September 1985), 41–53.

Stuart-Stubbs, Basil, and Carter, Ross. "Developing Library Service for Post-Secondary Education in British Columbia." Vancouver: N.p., 1976.

"Towards Improved Library/Community College Interaction: A Guide for Communication." Developed by chairpersons Allan Quigley, Pat Somerton, Bob Kreig. N.p., 1983.

Welwood, Ron J. "Management Indicators for British Columbia College and Institute Learning Resources Centres." N.p., 1981.

———. "Management Indicators for British Columbia College and Institute Learning Resources Centres: An Interim Report." N.p., 1980.

———. "Management Indicators for B.C. Learning Resource Centres," *Canadian Library Journal,* 39 (June 1982), 165–70.

Weweler, Johanna, and Oldridge, Edward. "Computerized Retrieval System for Audiovisual Materials: Saskatchewan Technical Institute," *Saskatchewan Library,* 32 (December 1978), 28–40.

Wright, Gordon H. "Co-operative Steps Toward a Library Network in Ontario," *Library Resources and Technical Services,* 20 (Fall 1976), 346–60.

————. "Developing the College Bibliocentre," *Ontario Library Review,* 55 (September 1971), 157–59.

————"Purchasing for Libraries: Advantages and Complexities of the CAATs' Co-operative Approach," *Canadian University and College,* 7 (January–February 1972), 23–26.

Zuraw, Cathy. "Analysis of 1983 CAAT External Borrower Policies," *COM-O-LIB,* 12 (December 1984), 2–15.

————. "Community College Copyright Policy Survey," *COM-O-LIB,* 13 (December 1985), 26–30.

THE COMMUNITY COLLEGE LIBRARY: A FACULTY PERSPECTIVE

William V. Costanzo

How does a community college library appear to its faculty? I asked colleagues at other campuses to describe the metaphor that comes most readily to mind. Here are some of their responses:

> Our library is like a supermarket. Almost all our wares are on open shelves in aisles plainly marked. We encourage patrons to help themselves, to feel free to pull an attractive title from the shelves to check its ingredients. [Borough of Manhattan Community College/CUNY]

> It's like a time-space machine. It allows people to travel forward and backward in time and to anywhere in physical or intellectual space that has been explored by the human mind. [Joan Hoffman, John Jay College of Criminal Justice]

> I think of a shopping mall. Not only do our students come for goods and services, they also come to socialize. The personal contact is as important as any knowledge that they seek. Or rather, it is the human face of knowledge that they find in our librarians, support staff, faculty, and other students. [Westchester Community College]

> It's like the hub of an automobile wheel. The various departments run out from it like spokes to the edge that moves forward, and back to it for power and energy to maintain momentum. It is connected to each part of the wheel (the university as a whole), moves in concert with the other wheels (a larger system of books and libraries),

yet maintains its own identity. [Ann Dobie, University of Southwestern Louisiana]

Like a popular rural train station, it's used often when the train goes through and many students are doing papers or studying for exams. At other times, it seems a quiet place. [Rosemary Lyons-Chase, Columbia-Greene Community College]

I'd compare our present library to Grand Central Station. Despite comings and goings, it is always full, rather hectic, functional . . . not conducive to contemplation, but busy, noisy, yet surprisingly still able to get most people off in the right direction. [LaGuardia Community College]

Whether the setting is urban or rural, north or south, the key concepts seem to be movement, activity, choice. One's overall impression is of vigorous diversity: many missions being served in a single place. Like most metaphors, these images bear connotations, traces of faculty beliefs of what a library ought to be. Should a library function as a marketplace? Should it be a peaceful haven from the busy world? Is its rightful place at the institutional center of learning, or as a station on the way to other destinations? Also embedded in these images are attitudes about librarians. Are they regarded today as members of an educational sales force? As gateways to knowledge? Stationmasters? Traffic officers? Cogs on a wheel?

Such faculty perceptions—and possibly misperceptions—are important because they help to shape the bonds between our libraries and the communities they serve. These perceptions also influence the professional identity of our librarians as they go about their daily work. My purpose in these pages is to address the issue of what faculty expect of librarians and college libraries. I want to consider the kinds of contact between faculty and librarians that typify their ongoing relationships and the roles which they perform for one another. I also want to look at specific areas where the roles appear to be most crucial: academic support, supplemental course work, educational technology, and faculty development. This will be primarily a personal view, the observations of one member

of the faculty at one community college. But it will be in-
formed by more than twenty years of teaching and conversing
with teachers across the country. What I hope will emerge
from this view are some useful thoughts on how we can work
together to provide more effective, meaningful support for
our students and each other in our mutual pursuit of learning.

Let me describe our college library as I see it in my mind. I
picture a large building, four stories high, at the center of a
medium-size suburban campus. Across a spacious, neatly
tended lawn, I see a handsome flagstone face, a collar of
azaleas and rhododendrons, a gathering of students walking,
reading, or conversing near the entrance. This image soon
gives way to an interior scene. There are familiar faces at the
checkout desk, on my left as I walk in. One librarian is sliding
a student's ID card through the optical scanner; another is
pulling a reserve folder from the vertical files. On my right, a
friendly voice calls hello from the information desk. I make a
mental note to stop by later for help with a research project
that I'm working on. Beyond, past several rows of carrels
lined with reference books and microfiche machines, more
librarians are serving students from the periodical collection.
I notice that the library's director is not scurrying about the
floor, so I assume she's at a meeting, or helping someone
upstairs, or hunched over her new computer in the office.
Further along, toward the central spiral staircase, is a large
stand of computer terminals. They have replaced the old
wooden card catalog with instant electronic access to the
library's entire holdings and a host of data bases. Although
these terminals are scattered all around the library, they are in
constant use.

In fact, the scene is teeming with activity. There are students at the counters, students in the reference section, students at the microfiche machines. Downstairs I know the
scene is just as busy. Some students are working on their
papers in the computer lab, some are huddled with peer
tutors in the Writing Center, others are checking out some
form of media from the Learning Center—a videotape of
Hamlet, a Beethoven recording, a laser-disc voyage to the
planets—while others are progressing through a math or
reading module with aid and comfort from the academic

support staff. Somewhere on the third floor, there is a space for quiet study. In an office, books are being ordered, and new holdings are being entered into an electronic data base. Activity, diversity, sundry paths to sundry ends.

What may be missing from this picture is the feeling of camaraderie which animates the building. The people here work well together; they like each other and communicate their cooperative spirit to the faculty and students. This spirit may owe something to the quality of interaction, which has always seemed remarkable to me. The staff are always consulting or filling in for one another. Many of the issues that affect their lives together are discussed at regular roundtable gatherings. They attend conferences together and encourage one another to take part in professional activities. Even the most onerous tasks are taken on collectively. One summer, when all the bookshelves had to be relocated, they held aerobic exercises every morning. Even non-librarians joined in.

I emphasize this climate of collective energy because I find that it exerts a strong magnetic force on the entire college. Hardly a day passes that I'm not drawn to the library for one reason or another. I may be placing course materials on reserve. I may need to do a search of ERIC titles to support a grant proposal. I may be meeting my Shakespeare class in the film projection room to analyze scenes from Olivier's *Richard III*. I may just be stopping in to ask the Writing Center tutors how my Basic Writing students are coming along or to consult about the latest desktop publishing software. Because it offers answers to so many needs, the building is a required station on my daily rounds.

There is another way that our librarians extend their reach. They serve on college-wide committees, get involved in student clubs, take on active roles in a variety of projects. Few are the meetings at which I don't see at least one face from the library staff. They tell me that they like to step out now and then, that they appreciate the chance to work with other faculty, students, and administrators, that they enjoy feeling part of something larger than the library. This is more than a vague feeling of inclusion. When librarians know what's going on, when they're on hand to help design the blueprints, the library remains a central, vital part of any institution's future.

Knowledge may be power, but being there is half the battle, twice the fun.

Are these conditions typical of two-year college libraries? Again, I asked my colleagues:

• *"How do students and faculty use your library to supplement regular class work?"* Most of the teachers I consulted take their students to the library for some form of orientation or library instruction. Often, these sessions are led by the library staff. Many teachers also keep required and supplementary readings at the library reserve desk. They report heavy use of periodicals, particularly those on microfilm, and note how changes in technology have altered patterns of retrieving information. With new machines arriving all the time, the need to orient each class and revise old courses becomes more and more essential.

• *"How does your library provide academic support to students, especially for basic skills?"* The libraries I polled run the gamut of academic support. At the urban college of LaGuardia, each basic-skills area has its own well-staffed, well-stocked lab; the library supplies materials and technology to assist students, tutors, and faculty. At the rural college of Columbia-Greene, facilities are limited to one quiet-study room, one classroom, and guidelines on specific study areas. Some institutions, like the University of Southwestern Louisiana (where a policy of open admissions assumes the mission of two-year colleges elsewhere), maintain departmental tutoring programs separate from the library. At Westchester, where tutorial services originally were located in the library for convenience, the proximity of these services has brought instructive benefits. What began as separate skills areas have grown together into a network of support which includes extensive audiovisual materials, computers, counseling, tutoring, and teaching in writing, reading, mathematics, and accounting. WCC's Academic Support Center, coordinated by the library, now covers an entire floor and involves peer tutors, technical assistants, regular faculty, a specialist in learning disabilities, and a staff of basic-skills professionals.

• *"What are your library's most effective uses of technology?"* The trend here is toward electronic storage and retrieval of information in a variety of media. While the core collection of each library may still consist of books, a growing number of schools are turning to computer-based systems for keeping track of books and non-print documents. Computer networks are linking libraries to each other and to national data bases, extending the reach of even the smallest schools. Nor is it uncommon for libraries to provide facilities for word processing, text scanning, and photocopying. Meanwhile, faculty report increasing uses of videocassettes, laser discs, computer software, CD texts, recorded books, hypermedia, and other technological innovations which blur traditional distinctions between visual and verbal texts.

It's getting harder to classify and store these successors to the printed book, especially for schools with modest budgets. As librarians and teachers struggle to keep up with the changes, they find themselves relying on each other more and more. In fact, technology may be responsible for bringing these two groups together in new ways. Before my school replaced the card catalog with a PALS computer system, most faculty could find their way around the stacks without much help. Suddenly, confronted by a new path to their destination, they needed guides. Our librarians became more indispensable than ever.

There may be an unwelcome side effect of this indispensability. What happens when the photocopier runs out of paper or the microfilm machine misbehaves or you need to set tabs on the electronic typewriter? In my school, you look for a librarian. So professionals who earned degrees in library science often find themselves taking on the role of technical assistant. I don't know how all librarians feel about the role. One told me that she's secretly flattered. After years of pleading ignorance to her auto mechanic, now she's mastering the mechanics of her trade. Another pointed out an unexpected benefit of technological expertise. When people ask for help with a machine, they're often willing to seek help in other matters. Once you've solved their immediate problem, you've gained a measure of trust. A bond is formed. Soon they may be asking for advice about the content of a paper or the meaning of an article. Technology becomes a bridge.

• *"What does your library do to help motivate faculty renewal?"* Responses to this question focused chiefly on the efforts of librarians to provide faculty with research materials. Book orders, extended borrowing privileges, information searches, and interlibrary loans were among the methods cited as support. These efforts all add up. I have always appreciated librarians who take an interest in my work. Whenever they set aside a book on my specialty or clip an article or get me titles from a data base, they are validating my efforts as a researcher. They are saying, in effect, that the topic I have chosen to investigate is worthy of investigation and that my work is worthy of support. Their respect is as important as the information they provide. In a community college, where the teaching load can be so draining and where faculty prestige is so precarious, respect is critical for genuine professional development. This is where I believe librarians can do the most good, by helping faculty to reestablish contact with their chosen discipline and, by strengthening the bonds that tie them to a field they love, renewing their professional identity.

• *"What advice, warnings, or words of inspiration do you have for the nation's community college librarians?"* The teachers I spoke with had much counsel to offer, from nuts and bolts to earnest generalities.

One teacher at a large inner-city school stressed the importance of maintaining a warm, personal environment. This is partly a matter of spatial design. Individuals feel lost in a huge, undifferentiated room. He suggested that librarians fashion lots of little nooks, using a few desks or tables to create opportunities for relatively quiet and productive isolation. He noted that students often like to form small study groups. Libraries ought to foster these instincts for collaborative learning whenever possible. Faculty from various departments can help by providing lists of essential books in their subject areas. When these books are arranged in clusters, especially near related tutorial centers, they can contribute to a sense of educational communities within the larger academic sphere. The same teacher stressed faculty presence and involvement. Some faculty find it useful to hold office hours in the library, where their students often feel more comfortable and where resources are close at hand. These faculty themselves feel more at home when librarians have consulted them about books in their fields and when the library has built strong collections in those fields. It also helps to display faculty publications and to confer seriously with faculty in each department when major changes in the library are being considered. It is through such partnerships that trust is built.

A teacher at a smaller, rural institution was more concerned about partnerships with the surrounding community. In a library with little inner space but strong links to regional and national resources through electronic networks and interlibrary loans, she felt it was important to develop ties to people and groups not ordinarily considered students. Thus, the community college library becomes an educational hub of the community, a window to the expanding world of information. The whole community becomes a citizenry of students in the school of lifelong learning.

Those who felt most strongly about the role of libraries and librarians had ardent words of encouragement. Recognizing the frustrations and problems of esteem that often face library professionals, they speak directly to the readers of this book:

> Don't isolate yourself from other faculty. Be active in the college community. Be aware of innovative teaching so that collection development is relevant to the curriculum. Do not allow the second class status usually accorded academic librarians to dampen your enthusiasm for your chosen field. [Borough of Manhattan CC]

> Though librarians seem to feel that they are insufficiently appreciated by the rest of the university staff, I can assure them that everyone is dependent on them for being able to carry on any research at all. Grateful comments may be seldom enunciated, but the work of the librarians is fundamental to the process of scholarship, and most professors know that, even if they fail to say so. [Ann Dobie, University of Southwestern Louisiana]

> Persist. Your task is an honorable one. [Rosemary Lyons-Chase, Columbia-Green Community College]

> The doors of a library are the doors to the magic of the outside world. Anything you can do to get students through those doors and to be aware of the strong force of "library power" is well worth the effort. Librarians can transform lives. [Joan Hoffman, John Jay College of Criminal Justice]

Librarians *can* transform lives. I have seen it happen again and again. A student hesitating in the margins of academia is drawn in by someone who cares about both students and the academic life. A member of the faculty who has lost touch with a subject in which she was once fervently engaged is inspired by someone who revives the spark of interest and fans the flame of self-esteem. Even when it's not a question of transforming lives, librarians can make a difference. They can make a difference in the way our students and our faculty solve specific academic problems. More important, they can make a difference in our attitudes. While providing supplementary course materials, they can help to validate a course of study. While supporting basic skills, they can address the fundamental motives and beliefs that underlie those skills. While supporting faculty development, they can help sustain the elements of personal growth that make professional growth possible and worthwhile. While offering the keys to new technologies, they can cope with the human needs that must come first. In the supermarket-station-hub-mall of the library, can there be a more important job?

TOWARDS EXCELLENCE IN BIBLIOGRAPHIC INSTRUCTION: A PRACTICAL APPROACH

Gloria B. Meisel

> The effectiveness of the library is of paramount impor-
> tance. . . . The centrality of a library/learning resources
> center in the educational mission of an institution de-
> serves more than rhetoric and must be supported by more
> than lip service. *An active and continuous program of biblio-*
> *graphic instruction is essential to realize this goal* [Simmons
> 4; emphasis added]. . . . Throughout the region my
> lectures about self-study, evaluation, and accreditation
> have included . . . a particular emphasis on bibliographic
> instruction as a primary tool to increase teaching effec-
> tiveness and student learning [Simmons 5].

For years bibliographic instruction librarians have be-
moaned the fact that no one outside of ourselves *really* understands or appreciates what it is that we *really* do.

At last, Howard Simmons, the executive director of the
Commission on Higher Education, Middle States Association
of Colleges and Schools, has publicly recognized this integral
component of library service. He has been a vocal and visible
champion of libraries in general and of bibliographic instruction programs in particular. The recognition of the importance of BI by a non-librarian, and an academically influential
one at that, may be exactly the acknowledgment BI librarians
and those trying to establish BI programs need.

Many libraries have successful programs in place. What
makes for such good programs? How do we know if we really
are succeeding? There are many established patterns and
many successful variations and innovations. The combination
of using established techniques and programs and addressing
local needs results in successful programs. Flexibility is the
key. The willingness to try something new, to discard that

which doesn't work or to keep and modify older techniques when necessary is integral to success.

Physical Structure/Restrictions

There is a commonality of possible physical locations used for BI. In some instances librarians still go out to the classrooms, and in fact, in a 1986 survey of head librarians at two-year colleges in New York State, 3 out of 29 respondents did classes this way (SUNY 1). This is obviously better than nothing, although far from optimal. Some campus programs have classes come to the library and work in the middle of the index area or reference stacks; some have open areas with chairs set up; some use available conference rooms which do double duty as library instruction classrooms; some are fortunate enough to have dedicated, lockable classrooms in which to teach and to store necessary equipment. The idea that such a session is being taught in a bona fide classroom seems to add a validity to the class that is missing in the other physical arenas. Librarians who have worked in both situations have noted that the students come into a classroom with different expectations, different demeanors, and different attention spans. This is not to suggest that valid, comprehensive library instruction is not attainable in other physical situations, but to many students a "real" classroom is synonomous with being "taught" a lesson, and they may be more amenable to learning in such a traditional setting.

Often the patterns of evolution of such programs are inexorably intertwined with buzz words, the jargon of the day: Information Literacy, Lifelong Learning, Critical Thinking, Information Anxiety, Articulation Programs, Learning Resource Centers (what happened to Libraries?), Library Instruction, Bibliographic Instruction, Library Use Instruction . . . Like myths and legends, these buzz words stem from basic truths and applications. We have shifted the focus from teaching techniques to learning styles; from libraries to learning resource centers; they are concepts not totally removed from one another, but the emphases are slightly different.

Information literacy is defined by Patricia Breivik as "a survival skill in the information age" (12). In some states there is movement to consider information literacy as a core requirement or as a component of basic-skills programs (Breivik 40). Making our students information literate—which really means making them aware of their *need* to be information literate not only in academia but in the world they will inhabit after leaving their campuses—is the obligation of all librarians. Whether we teach in a formal classroom setting or out on the reference floor, it is incumbent upon us to reinforce this awareness. How wonderful it would be if this were done all the way through, from the primary grades on!

General Practices

The traditional view of instruction in library use from the point of view of any teaching staff of the junior and senior high schools is that the basic skills were introduced and learned in the early grades. The view from the post-secondary instructors is that these skills have been reinforced in the junior high and high schools. This is not always the case for a variety of reasons, many the same as found on the community college level:

1. The skills may have been learned early on, but like any other skills, without constant use and reinforcement, they are quickly forgotten, and certainly not transferable as instructors would believe.

2. Teachers on any level are extremely reluctant to give up class time; the concept of integrating skills or analysis of the materials to be used for research often does not seem so important or relevant as the amount of information needed to be transferred in a relatively short period of time. This seems to be very short-sighted, in light of the American Library Association Presidential Committee on Information Literacy's definition of information-literate people as those who are able to "find, evaluate, and use information effectively." The report deems this ability a "survival skill in the information age" (6). Some educators think that schools must take the extra step to make sure that students are able to integrate what they have learned.

3. Many teachers assume that it's easy enough to use the library. The students will come in, and the librarian will take

a minute or two to refresh their memories on how and where to locate the needed information. That quick review is all that they need, or should need. After all, the teachers were able to satisfy their information needs that way when they were students. In reality, they only thought their needs were satisfied. Chances are that there was much more relevant information available which they were unable to unearth for lack of searching skills.

Considering how radically the information world has changed, we should be aware that more guidance is necessary for the students of today. High technology has permeated the information arena so it can be both easier and harder to get needed data. The student may be overwhelmed by the massive amounts of information retrieved from a search, and by the succeeding process of siphoning and assessing the data and possibly redefining the premise before it all becomes usable. Often, students searching a broad topic are unaware of the variety of information and ways of accessing the most pertinent data. To be *information literate* is to be able to look at and evaluate the mass of data as well as to be able to find it. A major component of information literacy is *critical thinking,* the concept of which should be integrated throughout the curriculum and the search process.

Competencies

In discussing searching procedures, the concept of competencies becomes important. Competency-based education generally implies setting standards of skills or concepts to be learned within a given time frame. Their importance is not to be dismissed. The concept of competency-based education on the post-secondary level has been explored by Carla Stoffle and Judith Pryor with specific regard to library instruction. They believe that instructional librarians must have an understanding of the concept so that they "are better able to relate their instructional programs to the needs of the institution and are prepared to adopt new approaches which may help improve the library instruction program itself" (57). The authors go on to discuss competency-based library instruction at various colleges and the different means of assessment, an important factor since BI programs "face heavy pressure for demonstration of their effectiveness" (Stoffle 65). They go on to state that such assessment is difficult at best and impossible without objectives. To this end, the list of basic competencies produced by the State University of New York Librarians' Association (SUNYLA) Task Force on Bibliographic Competencies appears at the end of this chapter. They are expressed in terms of behavioral objectives because the Task Force was interested in more than basic skills. Understanding of what is available and how those materials may or may not be appropriate for a particular information need was central to their charge.

As important as basic skills and competencies are in terms of information literacy, they should not be taught in a vacuum. If the student has nothing practical (in her/his perception) to be gained from a skills session, s/he will gain nothing. Statistics on what is remembered range from 30% (Paulson) to 42% (ALA) and worse, based on a sample group who were given material and tested one week following the lecture in question, 17% (ALA 7).

How do BI librarians, most of whom do reference desk service daily and have other duties within their libraries and institutions, impart the necessary amount of information to the students, hopefully with a degree of enthusiasm that will carry over, and in such a way as to have those students begin thinking of the process in evaluative terms and not just in how-to terms?

What the students are doing in those early years, writes Constance Mellon is "learning about the library" rather than "using the library" and she refers to this distinction as "the knowledge gap" ("Attitudes" 137).

The word "skills" is a constant throughout library literature. Actually, the how-to or library skills are learned with a fair degree of consistency in the lower grades wherever such programs are in place. Many school librarians use a workbook approach in teaching these skills, and often these workbooks are thorough and well thought out. In the junior high, middle, and high schools, teachers expect their students to have information-gathering abilities which students do not have. Not surprisingly, upper-level school librarians often find it difficult to counter those teacher expectations. Librarians face a high degree of resistance when they attempt to integrate structured library sessions within school curricula.

Mellon goes on to say that in her academic library experience in Tennessee certain things became obvious to her as they eventually do to all librarians dealing with college students. The transfer of knowledge from K-12 does not occur. Basic skills, terminology, and procedures, once learned, are by now forgotten. Forgetfulness may be due to one or more factors: the original learning may have taken place in the abstract, that is, without a specific, related project; it may have been learned in the very early grades and not reinforced throughout the public school experience; the student may be awed at the sheer size of the college library (or libraries, in some cases).

When we encounter new college students—or more realistically, students new to the college library—we must remember the following:

1. Students think everyone who works in the library is a librarian. This misconception is not limited to first-year students, and it persists across all socioeconomic and educational levels and across all types of libraries.

2. The students really do not want to do the paper/assignment/project at all; they would rather not be there, and they would rather get their information from the magazines and newspapers at home. They most emphatically do not want to hear another lecture about the card catalog (even if it *is* now automated, or fiche, or book) or about the green books *(Readers' Guide to Periodical Literature)!* This is not related to ability.

3. Many students (and other people) are afraid, or anxious, about using the library—any library—college or public. They may feel that everyone else understands everything; therefore, they are embarrassed to admit that they do not.

Anxiety and the Teaching-Learning Experience

Taking all of this into account, what are BI librarians to do? The anxiety factor is not one that is broadly addressed in the literature. Mellon is one academic librarian who has written about student attitudes and anxieties. "Information anxiety" is beginning to be written about, although not to a great degree. In a recent book by that name, Richard Saul Wurman addresses the problem of digesting and evaluating information relevant to the individual. One section is titled "Access Is the Antidote to Anxiety" (45). Although the material in the book is not geared to libraries (in fact, libraries are not mentioned, although reference books and organization of information are), there is much that is applicable to the problems our students face. If they can learn the lesson implicit in that section title, that access *is* the antidote to anxiety, they are on the way to success.

Also to be kept in mind is the complex non-traditional makeup of any community college student body. Returning adults, students in need of developmental services, veterans, foreign students, retirees—these form a rich, culturally and socially diverse population.

Now we have a sense of the library-awareness factors shaping the group of 30 or so students in each class. A big part of our job is to overturn the negative librarian image, relieve the anxieties, and impart a feeling of relevance and enthusiasm for the assignment. That's all! Next to this, the rest is easy. We have to begin by making connections with our faculty. We cannot do this alone. The instructor must give to the class a sense of the importance, relevance, and validity of this session. At many campuses it is a policy that no class will be taken for a BI session unless accompanied by the instructor. His/her presence lends credibility to the process, and even with this positive approach we have before us a difficult task. Sometimes we succeed and often we get halfway to our goals, but sometimes, we may never make substantive progress. Keep trying. We can start by talking with the students as they enter the room, and not necessarily about the assignment. Just talk. Make some kind of connection so that they don't see *the librarian*—they see a person.

The importance of that human connection cannot be overstated. Librarians no longer survey their territories with silencing finger to lips. Community college librarians are committed to public service and are obligated to have their campus constituencies recognize that fact.

After a BI program is established, every publicity tool available should be used to make the faculty aware of it. Even well-rooted programs need periodic reminders sent to class-room faculty so that they are not forgotten.

Once a program is under way another reality encroaches: most librarians have had no teacher training despite the fact that they teach in BI classes and on the reference floor. Schools of library service generally do not offer courses in BI, even though so many of the help-wanted ads require such experience. In a 1986 study by the Education and Library Use Committee of the Wisconsin Association of Academic Librarians, where 62% of the respondents were or had been involved in BI activities, only 16 individuals had received BI training as part of their MLS programs (Mandernack).

In a random look at graduate library school course-description catalogs in the greater New York area, it was found that Pratt offered courses in BI while Columbia, Queens, Rutgers, and LIU did not. This is not atypical.

The November 1989 issue of *American Libraries* had 33 classified advertisements listing some form of bibliographic instruction or library-user education as a job requirement. The April 1990 *College and Research Libraries News* listed 30. These numbers are significant. The reality is that although many colleges regard BI as a support service and the librarians as non-teaching faculty, librarians must use many of the same educational concepts and techniques as the classroom faculty. Since BI is not addressed in most library schools, it is part of on-the-job training.

As novices to teaching we concentrate in the beginning on transferring *all* of the information we feel students must have in a single 50-minute session. For most BI librarians, we have one 50-minute class period (less if attendance is taken, papers returned, tests announced, etc.) to transfer everything we think they have to know to complete their assignment successfully. Initially, getting through the period rather than really getting through to the students is of prime importance. After becoming somewhat comfortable with that, BI librarians usually progress to the next step, which is thinking about teaching techniques. In most library situations librarians new to BI should have a chance to observe experienced teachers before undertaking it themselves. One good introductory method is to have the new librarian team-teach with a more experienced person before actually taking a class her/himself.

This serves a second purpose: the more experienced librarian finds it nearly impossible to be observed without actually rethinking what s/he does in preparation for a class and in the presentation of the information. By reexamining techniques used and being forced, in a sense, to analyze them with another person, BI librarians can revitalize themselves.

We want to get the best to our students and to have them think about what they really need and to look carefully at what they get. Material on the Alaskan oil crisis published by the EPA will differ widely from Exxon's version. We want to encourage our students to find and evaluate sources, and we want to do this as enthusiastically and efficiently as possible, given our usual time constraints. The climb towards excellence must involve taking a sharp look at oneself periodically and making the commitment to change continually or eliminate those things which do not work, as well as working to enhance the things that do.

How do the students view us? We never see ourselves from the other side of the book cart, and one way to remedy this may be to have a class session videotaped. Media departments at many community colleges are equipped to do this. Two purposes are served here: 1) each librarian gets a chance to see what changes can and should be made; and 2) if this is done for a class in which several sections are doing the same assignment, the tape of information is on file for students who missed the session.

You might ask a trusted colleague to view the video with you and help critique it. In some cases the head of the department might be the person to watch with each individual. Look for the moments when everything seems to work. What did you do? Focus on the positive aspects, and it will make dealing with those less pleasing to you that much easier to discard or change. Realize that people respond differently to having extra lights, a camera, and floor wires surrounding them, so the beginning of the video might show a less-relaxed person than the at the middle or end.

Teaching styles are different. After some time, bibliographic instructors may feel burnout. There are ways to combat this. Ask your colleagues if you can sit in on their classes so that you can get fresh perspectives, and offer the same opportunity to them. Some people are quiet, methodical, careful in their approach; some are cheerleaders and try to rev up their classes; some respond well to questions or comments coming throughout the class; others prefer to take all questions at the end; some are loud; some are soft—all will have approaches somewhat different from one's own. Each can learn from the others and adapt specific techniques, emphases, or styles.

One area we are becoming more aware of these days is that of learning styles. We are moving from teaching techniques to what works best for different learners. We know that some respond best to visual stimuli, some to audio, most to hands-on, and all to repetition. If the repetition can be given in the variety of formats mentioned, there is a better-than-even chance that many students will be reached. Most of us do not have the luxury of a semester-long course where different learning styles and abilities of the students would be made clear within that framework. In our present situation we have a 40- to 50-minute period of time in which to look at a group, assess the individual learning styles, and adjust our lecture to accommodate what we see. This is virtually impossible. That is why a variety of techniques can work very well. There are steps that can be taken before the class comes in to get the feel and chemistry of the group:

1. What class are you teaching? With a basic English class the interest level may be low; a bit of creativity is in order. If the class is part of the students' curriculum, it is probably a more serious group who will be more responsive to a session on relevant resources.

2. Try to talk with the instructor before preparing for the class. Get her/his assessment of the students, their abilities and learning styles. Many will be quite willing to have such a discussion. It is to everyone's advantage to gear a session to a known quantity.

3. If a colleague has taught the instructor's students prior to your class, try to get input on the instructor's relationship with the students. None of these suggestions leads to a foolproof class, however. There may be two sections of the same class with the same professor on the same day with the same librarian and the same material; in one the chemistry may be just right and in the other it may be a disaster!

In thinking about learning styles (and personality types),

many may recall a little work published many years ago called *The Dot and the Line* by Norman Juster. Subtitled "A Romance in Higher Mathematics," it describes three basic personality types: the straightforward, dependable conservative line; the unkempt, unruly squiggle; and the frivolous dot who wants nothing more than to please that squiggle. Think about your students, or indeed any varied group of people brought together for a common purpose. They are all different. Psychotherapist Linda Zelizer's lecture, "How to Deal with Difficult People," concentrated on these geometric types in greater detail.

Her lecture had at its core the premise of people having geometrically oriented personalities, and that the people one finds difficult to deal are those with different "shape" characteristics from one's own. When entering that classroom we should be aware that we are facing a microcosm of linear and non-linear styles. Translation: Try to be aware of the differences in order to adapt the teaching styles to the learning/personality styles we face. Of course, these are not indelible, but the more awareness one has at the outset, the greater the chance of connecting. The shapes/styles described by Zelizer are:

1. *BOX:* Most resembles Juster's line. Very organized, straightforward, good at gathering information. [Are all librarians boxes? Hardly!] The box prefers structure; is task oriented.

2. *TRIANGLE:* Likes to be in charge, to be recognized; wants to get to the bottom line quickly.

3. *CIRCLE:* Likes harmony; wants to please; relationships take priority over facts and details.

4. *SQUIGGLY LINE:* Creative; does many things at once; often no follow through.

5. *RECTANGLE:* A box in the process of change; openness and receptivity are hallmarks; but inconsistent.

Recognize anyone? Awareness of these traits can be translated into recognition of different learning styles and may help to connect with more students. What does this mean for the BI librarian in terms of class preparation? Most probably talk about search strategies and processes and give good straightforward examples. This is great for the boxes in the room, and to some extent for the rectangles and the circles. What can be done for the triangle? Each of us can remember classes where all the questions centered on one student's paper, project, or problem. The triangle can be diverted and unilateral takeover prevented by (if at all possible) gearing some examples to that person's needs. Sometimes just being recognized individually satisfies such an individual, who may even stay tuned in the event that he or she is mentioned again. The circle, liking harmony, things pulled together, would appreciate hearing the agenda of what will be covered at the beginning of the session, and have it all tied up neatly at the end. If volunteers are asked for, circles and triangles will probably be the first hands up. The squiggle—well, the squiggle may or may not find a particular segment interesting enough to stay with. The squiggle needs variety, possibly a bit of entertainment.

Connecting with the students extends beyond the awareness of differences, however. A mix of lecture, audiovisuals, transparencies, board writing, and hands-on techniques will ensure that the most has been tried. We must vary our content and technique for ourselves, too. If we are bored and stale, how will the library lecture go over? It is not, after all, considered to be the most scintillating topic, except of course to a dedicated audience such as ourselves.

One aspect of learning styles is beyond our control—the time of day. Hopefully students register for courses given at the times of the day when they are most awake and alert. Some, especially in a community college, may have little choice. Many class times are determined by students' hours of employment, child care, etc. The best we can do is to sympathize with the difficulties some may have in getting to an 8 a.m. class or of needing a siesta after lunch instead of a 2 p.m. class.

Diversity of Students

When speaking to particular groups of students, librarians must be aware of above-average levels of anxiety. Among such groups are returning adult women, foreign students, students in need of remediation, and minority students. Some campuses have support services for adult women; librarians should be aware of such programs and offer to integrate library information on a slower, semester-long basis.

International students are often brought to the library as part of English-as-a-Second-Language classes or English-for-the-Foreign-Born classes. Often one 50-minute session is insufficient. Even if the classes run for longer periods, there is just so much that can be absorbed in one session. It is better to work with them in shorter periods so that one or two aspects of the library can be understood each time. One may find that foreign students seem to be reluctant to do searching and book or periodical retrieving on their own. In some countries libraries may not allow users to do so, while in others they are not expected to. When teaching such classes, librarians should make the effort to find out what countries are represented, how their libraries are organized, and how users go about getting the materials they need. We must also be aware of the tremendous ethnic minority growth in the United States: by the year 2000, 80% of the new population of the U.S. work force will be minorities, immigrants, or women, and at some point in the 21st century, whites will become a minority (Kappner 17). All of this can only translate to greater minority populations on community college and other campuses. Librarians must become aware of the range of cultural diversity of their students.

International students, as mentioned earlier, may follow different procedures in their native libraries, and may not have all of the services available as in an American college library. An important point to consider is that standards of acceptable and normal behavior in one place may not apply in another. Tesfai Kflu and Mary Loomba in their recent article note that personal space is a good example, since "North Americans feel comfortable with a conversational distance of about five feet [while] Arabs are used to a two-foot distance" (527). A median comfort zone has to be established, somehow, for all. Patience and continued willingness and offers of assistance will go far to set good international relations.

Minority students reflect another aspect of cultural diversity. Differences occur from one minority group to another and from one cultural group to another. Above all, according to Kflu and Loomba, "avoid stereotyped attitudes about the abilities and achievements of these students"; they can certainly benefit from intensive bibliographic instruction as well as any other group (526). Again, patience, willingness to help, and a ready smile together with a well-structured BI program for these groups of students can achieve for them a degree of comfort, expertise, and understanding of the use of their college library.

Another campus group that can benefit from a library session is the college support staff. Everyone from secretaries to mail clerks to maintenance workers should know what is available to them. Course-related instruction is not applicable, but a general introduction to the LRC and its materials and personnel is recommended. This allows college staff from various parts of the campus to put faces to the names and voices they've been dealing with and to become users and advocates of the LRC. Many are continuing their educations and make good use of the resources after an introductory session. A session such as this enables them to be less anxious about asking for help later on. Some major change, such as the installation of an on-line catalog, for example, is an excellent opportunity for introducing staff to the library.

Much discussion is given to the concept of outreach in many areas, and college libraries in general and community colleges in particular are no exceptions to that practice. Bibliographic instruction classes are offered to high school classes nationwide. A State University of New York (SUNY) survey, done in 1986 indicated that 37 of the 45 respondents offered varying degrees of college library orientation/instruction for high school juniors and/or seniors (1). This type of articulation addresses several areas:

1. *Anxiety:* That word is back again! A high school junior or senior, accustomed to a one-room high school library is simply unprepared for a university library (or libraries), or even a smaller community college library. In most cases, even the three often heard (but less often understood) words—*Dewey decimal system*—are missing from most college libraries. Many freshmen find the library such a threat that they delay using it or worse, never use it.

2. *Need:* Many high school students need a library with

longer hours and/or a greater diversity of specialized print and non-print materials than may be available in their public or school libraries.

3. *Recruitment:* The LRC may be an underrated tool. Let your administration know what you are doing. Many high schools in every area have students coming to your college; let them have a preview of how welcoming you can be and they will be more responsive when they begin as freshmen. Ask your public relations office to give you college folders to hand out. Anything that will increase the comfort zones of prospective students should be done.

Westchester Community College

The genesis of BI at WCC goes back to the 1950s when there were two librarians on staff in a large room in the technology building. In addition to reference work, ordering, and cataloging, they undertook the important task of library instruction for students and began in the old-fashioned way: "toting." One librarian did all the classes. She would speak to the instructor, find out what the class was doing, stuff as much as possible into a canvas bag, and go out to the classroom.

At WCC the program grew gradually, gaining popularity and validity among the faculty by word of mouth, and by the constant visibility of the librarians. This method has been called by the department chair, Rosanne Kalick, LBGOOTB (à la Thomas Peters in *A Passion for Excellence).* The translation: Librarianship By Getting Out Of The Building.

Over the years the library grew, and in 1968 we had our own building. Space was found for library instruction at the back of the reference stacks. As committed as the librarians were to bibliographic instruction, something as radical as a separate, formal classroom was not yet thought of. As of twelve years ago, the space held approximately 35 chairs, 40-plus when necessary for the larger business and psychology classes ("held" is a euphemism for spilling out onto the floor and into the telephone alcove), a blackboard, and an overhead projector and was known as the "Teaching Area."

As a result of the long-range planning committee of the

now-renamed Library and Learning Resource Center (getting anyone but the librarians to call it that took some doing), we moved BI to another floor to be housed in a partitioned area. It held the same number of chairs and could accommodate the same amount of equipment but was now a separate "class-room" since it was safe from the distractions of other students walking by and waving.

The next step in our physical evolution brings us to the present. A classroom in the LRC is finally ours! We have a door that can be closed and locked when not in use, a chalkboard, a marker board, a bookcase, and an on-line projector and screen to teach the use of the on-line catalog.

Commitment

We certainly have come a long way, but we are not there yet. One thing we realize as we strive towards excellence in any endeavor is that we will never reach the end. We just continue to rethink our goals and to set them higher. This means constant change. Tom Peters, in his book *Thriving on Chaos,* notes that "change must become the norm, not cause for alarm" (464). How else are we to keep ourselves fresh, awake, and enthusiastic about a function we're called upon to perform over and over? When a BI class is over, ask yourself (or your students), "What worked?" Question that which did and that which didn't. Then ask, as Peters does, "What's next?" (465).

Indeed, what's next for us can be found by looking at general education trends. In the last few years educators have been advocating collaborative learning as a method of getting more students involved. This can easily work in a semester-long class that meets several times a week, but having it work in a one-shot bibliographic instruction session seemed highly improbable. But, in looking at what we are trying to get across to students and knowing that an interaction and an investment of themselves in the process is what is needed, we thought an experiment was worthwhile. It worked! It takes longer to prepare a class and materials and is not relevant in all situations, but there are many instances where the time spent is worth the return. Here are two brief examples: 1) Instead of telling a class about all of the amazing material in the reference books on your cart, separate the students into groups of three and four, give each group a book, give them three-to-five minutes to discuss it among themselves and have each group's (pre-chosen or volunteered) reporter give a one-minute talk about it. The first group's reporter needs the most prompting; 2) In a class that must use professional journals, you might begin by asking what they read at home, who writes for those magazines, how long the articles run, etc. Give each group one or two journals to look at for the next few minutes and as in the first example, let them run with it. If you do not wish to have a reporter, you can elicit responses by asking specific questions about the material. This all takes more class time than you may feel you can give up, but if it can be managed, the results are well worth it. They learn and retain more with a hands-on approach and the anxiety of being singled out is lessened. Always ask yourself, "Might this work? Shall I take the chance?" The answer is always a resounding "Yes." If you do not take the chance, neither you nor the students will ever know if it can work.

We must always take the extra step, go beyond the merely serviceable. Our students really are aware of any extra interest and concern shown to them. Directly related to this is our obligation to our students to make the connection with faculty and encourage them to bring their classes to the LRC whenever an information-gathering project is assigned. Taking on more classes is a lot of work, but it is more work to teach 30 individuals at the reference desk than 30 in one class. The students benefit since we've had time to organize and prepare the most relevant resources for their assignment. The faculty benefit from a more readable, comprehensive final paper. Sometimes even when they agree to the premise, faculty are still reluctant to give up necessary class hours, particularly in states where time can be lost to snow days as well. Never stop trying. Interest can be raised in many ways: ask faculty for their much-needed help in weeding their areas of expertise, and use some of the time to talk about the program; send letters each semester reminding them of your availability; inform them of new, relevant subject materials;

let them know about policy changes, etc. Invite all new faculty—full-time and adjuncts—each semester for an introduction to and tour of the facilities. Be sure to provide them with CARE packages of information about services and necessary names and telephone numbers. Try arranging meetings with various departments, in the LRC if possible. Host coffees or have a campus-wide party whenever something major takes place, such as the installation of an on-line catalog. Be visible and be vocal. Establish your presence in the college community whenever possible by taking part in committees and campus activities. Do not give up; we know what our LRCs have to offer and in time many of your faculty will, too.

At Westchester Community College our library faculty is very active on campus committees; we are well represented on faculty senate committees, and two librarians are club advisors; one meets students while teaching a Great Books course and one by teaching photography in the Community Services division. We have asked faculty to come and speak to us at monthly staff meetings and at the staff development day we hold prior to each semester. The chair of the Theatre Department spoke to us about stage presence—not theatrics, but how to keep the students' attention focused on the material instead of the miscellany of the environment. On the basis of this discussion we changed the physical arrangement of our chairs and equipment. Your classroom-teaching colleagues will be happy to help and pleased to be asked.

We have invited the associate deans of each division to speak with us about their curricula and how we can better integrate our services and resources; we invited the registrar to discuss the (then) upcoming computerized registration and the ramifications for the LRC's overdues process. All of this is information we need, and these meetings afford us both the means of getting information and the opportunity to let others on campus know what we have to offer.

Bibliographic instruction librarians can develop special relationships with high-risk-student groups, which can be reached by working with faculty and program coordinators. These groups are considered high risk in that the fear or history of failure has been great. We are trying to reduce the fear as well as reverse the cycle of failure. We have been able to do that to a small degree although it sometimes feels like a mental and emotional combat zone, but the successes make it well worth the effort.

In some groups, such as returning adult women, we find an above-average level of anxiety. On our campus a Women's Forum is in place, run by a counselor. As part of their introduction to the college, they are brought onto the campus one week before classes begin. Part of the day is a two-hour library segment The women bring their own lunch; we provide coffee, cider, cookies, and after a short welcome they eat while watching the film *Turning Points.* The film deals with three (real) adult women who have returned to school on the community college level for different reasons. A library is even shown in this film. Afterward the women are given a floor plan and talked through and walked through on a tour. The Women's Forum and the Displaced Homemakers (women in transition from home to workplace) are the only groups that get a tour and a talk in a vacuum, that is to say, without an assignment. They will get library instruction in those classes which do come to the LRC; in addition, or to accommodate those who would not get here that way, we teach a 90-minute general research-strategies class as part of a three-session program in conjunction with the English and Reading Departments. We also offer a separate 90-minute lesson on the on-line catalog. This has helped many develop a greater confidence in dealing with the new technologies.

Students in the developmental reading classes also need special attention. Libraries are not familiar places to them, yet they are unafraid, as a whole, of using the on-line catalog. They, of course, are part of the video generation and more comfortable with the small screen than with a blank piece of paper or a card file. This is a particularly important group in that part of their success may depend on being comfortable enough to ask any question without the fear of being laughed at or thought dumb. We strive to make them comfortable in the library. If they have success here, and manage to shed some of that library anxiety at the same time, that is our success as well.

One of the small things that can help make lasting connections with these high-risk groups is to remember as many students' names as possible. It is meaningful to students to find out that a faculty member really knows who they are. Peters and Waterman made note of just this kind of effort in their book *In Search of Excellence* (xvii).

Librarians *must* get to know the Reading Department faculty. We got to know them easily because their offices and classrooms were in the LRC. At the inception of the program, there was little or no use of the library. At best (or worst) their students were sent down en masse to find a non-fiction book. The library staff tried to remedy this for some time, albeit unsuccessfully. In this case it took a change of faculty to bring the two areas together. Over the last ten years we have worked together to develop workable assignments. We have two levels of reading classes, and different assignments have been created for each, and changed and modified and changed again over the years. The students in all of the classes on the first level must use a standard desk dictionary to look up a person, a country, and a word. Each student then picks one of the three and looks it up in the on-line catalog. A worksheet is provided for them to answer specific questions about the books they find and their methods of searching.

The second-level students come to the LRC twice during the semester. Their first assignment is the standard birthday assignment, in which they get to use the microfilm machines. We have made a very brief in-house video on how to load the machines, and if a VCR is available during the class session we show it. Perhaps one day we can have a dedicated VCR and make more use of such videos. This takes away part of the frustration of the second assignment: to find one book and two magazine articles on a specific topic. They generally use the topics of television, work, and the family. They are taught how and why to narrow the topic. For those who need magazines in microfilm format it is non-threatening, since they have already had success in that area. College librarians are working with high school students in outreach programs. Most are informal although some do have a formal structure and requirements. As noted earlier, BI is a useful mechanism for introducing these students to a college library and more sophisticated resources, and a useful survival tool for us— many will use our library anyway. High schools use the programs for their advanced placement classes, but should be encouraged to bring the non-AP students, too, for as one student put it, the others will get to that information anyway, but it's the rest of the us that need it. The reality is that the non-AP students will be more likely to enter the community college, and an extra visit to the LRC can be a definite plus. Our program began informally: our acquisitions librarian belonged to a book group in which one of the members was a high school English teacher. She called, and the program began. The local high school librarians were invited to a reception to introduce them to the program. We now see several classes a semester during the slow times and would like to see the program grow.

This collaborative effort is part of a larger trend. Community colleges in general have been greatly involved in such programs (Mabry 48-49). The library connection is a logical component in this pattern.

The members of Mainstream and the college support staff also come to general orientations. Several years ago the support staff were invited to brown-bag it to a general library orientation. We had three packed sessions. When our on-line catalog was installed, we offered a second series of sessions. This time they were permitted to use one hour of college time for the two-hour class. We are in the process of scheduling new classes on the enhancements of the on-line catalog as well as on advanced searching techniques. The other group—Mainstream—is made up of older adults. They sign up for two-hour sessions in the use of the on-line catalog. They are eager to learn and do so without the impetus of an assignment.

This has been a brief overview of the instructional-service program at WCC. It is probably not very different from other programs for which there has been support from all levels of the administration. The Learning Resource Center at WCC has been fortunate to have that support and to have as associate dean of our academic division the person who began here as head librarian. We set minimum requirements in scheduling BI classes, for example, the class must be course related; it must be booked one and one-half to two weeks in advance; and the instructor must accompany the class. These stipulations are to make the classes more meaningful and valid for the students we teach. Our college president and administrative heads have all been strong supporters of the library and its services. Certainly libraries without that support have a very different story to tell.

We can offer our support to our colleagues still attempting to make their programs a reality and to those trying to enhance existing ones.

Do not be afraid to take risks. Patience, perseverance, and a strong belief in what can be accomplished are key elements in successful efforts. Indeed, according to the current standards for community college libraries as set by the Association of College and Research Libraries, "Learning resources exist to facilitate and improve learning by supporting and expanding classroom instruction and to perform the instructional function of teaching students the information-seeking skills for self-directed studies and life-long learning" ("Standards" 761). We are being noticed; with people like Howard Simmons recognizing the importance of what we do, our place in the teaching-learning process is becoming secure.

Recommended Library Skills and Competencies for Graduates of Two-Year Colleges in New York State

PREPARED BY THE SUNYLA BIBLIOGRAPHIC COMPETENCIES TASK FORCE, 1988

A. Given a problem, the student will identify and analyze an information need, consulting a reference librarian as needed.
   1. The student will identify and clearly state major topics in a research question (information need).
   2. The student will determine the type of information needed, i.e.,
      a. popular or scholarly
      b. primary, secondary
      c. current or retrospective
      d. overview, statistical, critical, biographical, etc.
   3. The student will translate the question into subject headings and/or keywords used in reference sources.
   4. The student will broaden and narrow a topic as necessary, choosing relevant subject headings.

B. Given an information need, the student will develop a search strategy to satisfy the need.
   1. The student will identify types of sources appropriate to satisfy specific information needs, i.e., specific reference sources, indexes, etc.
   2. The student will keep a record of sources used.
   3. The student will be able to modify the search strategy as necessary.

C. The student will demonstrate the ability to use library resources to carry out the search strategy.
   1. The student will utilize and apply the services, policies, and procedures of the library.
   2. The student will be able to locate materials in the library (*physical* arrangement).
   3. The student will effectively utilize the library's catalog in any form (card catalog, on-line, COM, CD-ROM).
   4. The student will be able to locate an item in the library by using the call number.
   5. The student will use the information found in a book's table of contents, index, and/or bibliography to locate information.
   6. The student will select appropriate common reference tools, such as almanacs, atlases, encyclopedias, and dictionaries, etc., to satisfy an information need.
   7. The student will identify and use specialized reference books and journals, and, where available, government documents in a field of study.
   8. The student will use a periodical index and interpret a citation.
   9. The student will locate a periodical in the library using a periodicals holdings list.
   10. The student will use microforms, non-print materials, and/or computer software with appropriate equipment as needed to satisfy an information need.
   11. The student will recognize the availability and usefulness of both in-house and commercial data bases (dependent on library resources available).
   12. The student will consider sources outside the college library, including interlibrary loan, as well as other libraries and agencies.

D. The student will demonstrate the ability to analyze and evaluate whether the information located will satisfy his/her information need.

E. The student will be able to define the role of the reference librarian for satisfying his/her information need(s).

List of Works Cited

American Library Association Presidential Committee on Information Literacy. *Final Report.* Chicago: American Library Association, 1989.

Bodi, Sonia. "Teaching Effectiveness and Bibliographic Instruction: The Relevance of Learning Styles." *College and Research Libraries* (1990):113–119.

Breivik, Patricia Senn, and E. Gordon Gee. *Information Literacy.* New York: Macmillan, 1989.

Juster, Norman. *The Dot and the Line.* New York: Random House, 1963.

Kappner, Augusta Souza. "Creating Something to Celebrate." *Community, Technical, and Junior College Journal* December/January 1990–1991:16–21.

Kflu, Tesfai, and Mary Loomba. "Academic Libraries and the Culturally Diverse Student Population." *College and Research Libraries News* June 1990:524–527.

Mabry, Theo. "The High School/Community College Connection: An ERIC Review." *Community College Review* 16(Winter 1988):48–55.

Mancher, Carolyn. "Connecting with Your Audience." *College Teaching* 37(1989):46–48.

Mandernack, Scott B. "An Assessment of Education and Training Needs for Bibliographic Instruction Librarians." *Journal of Education for Library and Information Science* 30(Winter 1990):193–205.

Meisel, Gloria, and Rosanne Kalick. "Marketing Bibliographic Instruction Through Improved Communication." *Community and Junior College Libraries* 2(Spring 1984):21–30.

Mellon, Constance. "Attitudes: The Forgotten Dimension in Library Instruction." *Library Journal* 1 September 1988:137–139.

Mellon, Constance. "Library Anxiety: A Grounded Theory and Its Development." *College and Research Libraries* 47(1986):160–165.

Paulson, Terry. "Managing Motivation." Address, National Learning Resources Conference, San Francisco, 21 February 1990.

Peters, Thomas J., and Robert H. Waterman, Jr. *In Search of Excellence*. New York: Harper, 1982.

Peters, Tom. *Thriving on Chaos*. New York: Knopf, 1987.

Peters, Tom, and Nancy Austin. *A Passion for Excellence*. New York: Random House, 1985.

Simmons, Howard. "An Accreditor's Perspective: Bibliographic Instruction as a Tool for Learning." Speech, Borough of Manhattan Community College, 19 May 1989.

"Standards for Community, Junior and Technical College Learning Resources Programs." *College and Research Libraries News* 51(September 1990):757–767.

State University of New York. Head Librarians. *Survey on Bibliographic Instruction*. New York, May 1986.

Stoffle, Carla J. and Judith M. Pryor. "Competency-Based Education and Library Instruction." *Library Trends* 29 (Summer 1980): 55–67.

Wurman, Richard Saul. *Information Anxiety*. New York: Doubleday, 1989.

IDENTITY OF COMMUNITY COLLEGE LRCs: DIVERGENT OR CONVERGENT?

Margaret Holleman and Annette Peretz

Since the post–World War II expansion of community colleges, their libraries/LRCs have been as unique among academic libraries as the institution has been unique in higher education. Recent trends in higher education and society, however, have caused LRCs to develop closer links and likenesses to other types of libraries.

Unique Nature of Learning Resources Centers

Learning resources programs have been innovative in responding to the broad mission of the two-year college: its "open door" philosophy and diverse enrollments, its emphasis on teaching rather than research, and its responsiveness to the changing needs of the local community.

This is reflected in the nature of LRC clientele, collections, staffs, and facilities; emphases on audiovisual, computer, and instructional technologies; and involvement in the college's instructional programs. The recently revised standards for two-year college LRCs highlight other major distinctions in philosophy and organizational structure: the integration of library and audiovisual services and a systems approach to applying all available resources—wherever housed—to providing learning materials and support for experimental instructional techniques and professional development.

Clientele
After World War II thousands of men and women returned from military or defense assignments and needed to be reeducated for peacetime employment. Technologies developed

during the war had become part of the industrial landscape. Postsecondary education was necessary for high school graduates to prepare them for new fields of employment. Community colleges were the educational institutions open without prerequisites or restrictions to all members of the community. The post-war influx of GIs and minorities into two-year colleges marked the beginning of increasing enrollments of non-traditional students, including the physically challenged; those having job or family responsibilities; the economically, culturally, or academically disadvantaged; reentry women; non-native speakers; and prisoners. According to AACJC, the typical community college student today is female, part-time, older (average age twenty-nine), employed at least part-time, and taking course work to gain employment or for job training.

Collections

Materials in community college libraries tend to be as diverse as the enrollments and curricula they support. Wartime instructional techniques had demonstrated the value of non-print ancillary materials, such as films and slides, to reinforce learning.

The multi-media collections which LRCs have established to accommodate different learning and teaching styles must be continuously updated. However, a combination of recent trends—rapid obsolescence of audiovisual materials, expensive new information technologies, higher costs and lower printing runs of publications (particularly serials), and diminished institutional funding and enrollments—have made it difficult for LRCs to keep pace.

LRCs are now expected to acquire microcomputer software, CD music recordings, CD-ROM products, VHS tapes, and laser discs. Indeed, bibliographic networks, telecommunications systems, and on-line or CD-ROM data bases (often with summaries of the full text of documents) have given users in even the smaller and more remote facilities dramatically expanded access to the world of information.

Learning resources programs frequently include media development departments which help faculty to integrate media into courses and also to design and develop audiovisual materials unavailable commercially. LRCs also provide users with various types of audiovisual equipment, such as film, film-strip, and slide projectors, VCRs, microcomputers, micro-form reader-printers, and compact disc drives to support the multi-media collections.

Librarians acquire not only the traditional materials to support transfer and general education but specialized items, such as high-interest/low-difficulty-level materials for reme-dial and literacy classes and materials to support women's, ethnic, ESL, and international studies and career counseling. They also provide curricular support for such diverse occupa-tional programs as allied health; automotive, air-conditioning, and aircraft repair; construction, electronics, and agricultural technologies; and legal, medical, library, and classroom assist-ing. Indeed, the collection in each LRC reflects the needs of its community.

Community college districts, such as Coast, Dallas, and Miami-Dade, and the Southern California Consortium for Community College Television, have been foremost in the nation in the production of high-quality, widely used tele-courses. In order to afford the lease and purchase of such expensive instructional materials as telecourses, groups of community college LRCs around the country have formed cooperatives.

NILRC—Northern Illinois Learning Resources Coopera-tive—is the successful prototype. NILRC has co-produced a number of high-interest telecourses in order to make them freely available to members. NILRC also negotiates purchase and lease agreements for less popular telecourses, splitting the costs among the requesting members, and establishes group contracts for such things as projector lamps, library supplies, and CD-ROM products. NILRC also promotes staff development activities, alternating with the Learning Re-sources Association of California Community Colleges (LRACCC) in sponsoring a National Learning Resources Conference every eighteen months.

Staff

Many of the libraries, such as that at Mesa Community College (Arizona), train library and media technical assistants for important supportive roles in LRCs, many of which have limited professional staffing. Many LRCs also incorporate learning centers which offer developmental courses and/or tutoring, primarily for writing, reading, and mathematics, but also for other subjects, such as accounting, languages, and the natural and physical sciences. LRC staff tend—of necessity— to be generalists rather than specialists. Most are highly service-oriented, operating strong public relations programs and designing inviting, comfortable facilities for students, many of whom initially find libraries and their institutions intimidating.

LRC staff are especially sensitive to the needs of nontraditional students. According to The National Center for Education Statistics, approximately 53% of undergraduate minorities are enrolled in community colleges (193–194). LRCs actively support programs such as ESL; developmental, international, ethnic, and women's studies; and interpreter training; and provide handicapped students with specialized equipment.

The Department of Library/Learning Resources at Bronx Community College in New York City illustrates LRC support for non-traditional students. A two-building model, its library is traditional in functions and services, providing print material and microfilms which support curricular and recreational needs, a law library which supports a paralegal program and utilizes WESTLAW on-line services, and a Kurzweil reader which assists visually impaired students.

The library operates a Learning Center in an adjacent building. There LRC staff offer a variety of services: orientation workshops; walk-in tutoring; audiovisual workstations which are used by 200 to 500 students each day; and a reserve instructional-materials collection. The LRC also provides a Braillewriter, specialized voice-activated audio and computer equipment, and amplification apparatus for clients with visual or auditory impairments.

Administratively discrete but contiguous with the Learning Center is a Student Support Center which provides legal and social services, academic-skills counseling, learning-disabilities evaluation, and assistance with writing, reading, ESL, and study skills. The center also operates the college's centralized tutoring program. Learning Center librarians identify students who may benefit from the services of the learning-skills counselors of the Student Support Center and make personal referrals. Students feel a close connection and use both facilities comfortably.

Involvement in Instruction

Professional staff take proactive roles in the instructional programs of the colleges. Most LRCs have a representative on the college's curriculum committee. And many hire technologists to help faculty design courses and develop innovative teaching strategies.

The entire program at the Spring Creek Campus of Collin County Community College (Plano, Texas), for instance, is literally and figuratively designed around the LRC. One of the newest facilities in the country, it focuses on experiential, active learning. A lab component in all disciplines involves students in projects which engage them in inquiry, critical analysis, synthesis, and problem solving. Students complete many of the lab projects in the Alternative Learning Center (ALC) of the LRC. For instance, they can use film clips from the *Video Encyclopedia of the Twentieth Century* to view and evaluate historical events and to produce their own videotapes. Lab components may also consist of any of the annual "Connections" series of cross-disciplinary public events— speakers, films, field trips, or performances—sponsored by the ALC (Ducote, Tibbals, and Prouty 65,68).

Technologists at the LRC at Tulsa Junior College assist faculty with interactive computer authoring systems and operate a centralized state data bank of instructional (CAI) courseware which can be accessed electronically by anyone in the country. Instructional technologists at the Jackson Community College (Michigan) LRC have created a professional-development "drop-in" center. Faculty and staff find assistance there in selecting and completing mediated programs in such areas as management techniques, teaching strategies, emerging technologies, college policies and procedures, wellness, and program planning and budgeting. College faculty and staff help select these topics, design the programs, and evaluate the center, and the college rewards their participation (Major 41–42).

The LRC at Austin Community College has developed a model program for assisting developmental education students, and the LRC at the College of DuPage works closely with the college's literacy education program. Austin's program integrates library-skills instruction into various developmental classes, librarians working closely with instructors. Many community college LRCs are integrating various levels of library instruction into college classes and many, such as the one at the Auraria Campus of Denver Community College, are teaching library research as a problem-solving process and are having students critically evaluate the primary and secondary sources they use.

The Library Media Resource Center at Fiorello LaGuardia Community College in New York offers a heavily enrolled three-credit course, Information Strategies, which introduces students to the nature and uses of information sources for study and problem solving. A hands-on course, it includes application of these strategies by using advanced research technologies.

Austin's LRC, like many others around the country, has also designed effective methods for providing learning resources to support the college's outreach and distance education programs. LRC staff provide on-line reference, courier, fax, and interlibrary loan services to widespread off-campus locations. They have also established agreements with area public and high-school libraries to provide college students with basic support collections and services.

In 1988 the Community College Association for Instruction and Technology (CCAIT) and the Community and Junior College Libraries Section (CJCLS) of the Association of College and Research Libraries sponsored a prototype library teleconference on CD-ROM technology. Intended for the professional development of LRC staff in rural and remote areas, the teleconference was viewed by approximately 6,000 people at 335 multi-type receiving sites across the nation. It was telecast from Oakton Community College in Des Plaines, Illinois. The College of DuPage produced a follow-up teleconference in 1989.

Facilities

Normally quite diverse in organizational structure, two-year college learning resources programs are increasingly becoming integrated technology centers to provide total information service. Cuyahoga and Dallas County Community Colleges have opened new resource centers which house instructional delivery and distribution networks. The new Technical Resource Center (TRC) at Greenville Technical College (South Carolina) provides a unique mix of information, programming, and instruction, using an extensive roster of networks and systems to connect the college to the entire community.

Greenville's TRC incorporates a library, on-line computer system, multi-purpose television studio, 250-seat auditorium for teleconferences, media production facility, staff/faculty training and curriculum center, a 110-seat computer-assisted learning lab, and low-power, closed-circuit (ITFS), UHF open-broadcast, and cable television for distance education. TRC staff coordinate the local delivery of governmental on-line research through a NASA affiliate. In addition to an automated library system, the TRC also offers users many CD-ROM indexes and interactive video disc materials.

Greenville Tech will also serve as headquarters for a proposed Greenville Education Network, transmitting quality educational and cultural programming around the clock to all college centers, the local public library, museum, and science centers, and all county residences, governmental offices, and school districts.

A new campus in the Maricopa County Community College District—Estrella Mountain—will be built around a similar integrated library center which will house the library, media services, and microcomputer, literacy, and innovation centers, and will serve as a model for subsequently redesigning the LRCs at the other MCCCD colleges in Phoenix, Arizona.

New Emphases and Linkages for LRCs

Such multi-type library cooperation as is involved in Tulsa's instructional courseware data bank, the CD-ROM teleconferences, and support agreements for outreach and distance education programs mark a shift to more cooperative ventures and linkages.

Joint-Use Agreements
Most community college LRCs were originally high school libraries shared by the college. The current high cost of

providing LRC facilities and the presence on many community college campuses of university centers and alternative high schools has made such joint-use ventures popular again. LRC librarians have forged strong liaisons with high school faculty and students in order to assist with their bibliographic instruction and research projects.

In addition to being more efficient and cost-effective, shared-use facilities and collections provide increased access to information for all users through union lists of holdings on on-line public-access catalogs. Florida has eight examples of community college joint-library-use agreements with universities, two with high schools, and two with public libraries. Other examples exist in Texas, North Carolina, Colorado, Montana, Arkansas, and Tennessee.

These joint-use agreements exhibit a wide variety of patterns of sharing of responsibility for governance, staffing, acquisitions, technical services, and general operations. Cost allocations are generally based on the respective student head counts of the participating institutions. In creating such agreements cooperating libraries must carefully assess their differing missions, clientele, and needs (Anderson).

Multi-type Library Cooperation

At the 1990 ALA Convention the Community and Junior College Libraries Section of ACRL sponsored a presentation on multi-type library cooperation. Speakers described the participation of the LRCs at four Illinois community colleges—Oakton, Kankakee, Triton, and Joliet—in Illinet-Online (IO). They are among thirty-three academic libraries sharing a local public access catalog which taps into a statewide data base of 4.5 million records. And Delta College (Michigan) is part of a sixteen-member regional consortium which shares CLSI's automated library system from a central location.

In New York State, clients at the Westchester Community College library use PALS (Public Access Library System) terminals to access an automated county-wide data base. Members include academic, public, and school libraries. As is the case in many states, the state university is the hub from which many linking programs radiate. The State University of New York (SUNY) sponsors a satellite group (SUNYSAT) which provides downlink capabilities for sixty-four colleges, thirty of which are community colleges. The state is dotted as well with consortia of regional and community colleges which have formed their own partnerships for participation in distance-learning services, cooperative purchases, and resource sharing. SUNY Central has also provided the opportunity for state postsecondary institutions to order and receive computer-generated cataloging from their Central OCLC Bureau.

An urban higher education system, the City University of New York provides open access to all CUNY faculty and students in the system regardless of their home campus. Currently all colleges in the system are having their libraries/ LRCs connected with the installation of the NOTIS automated library system, which will link the holdings of ten senior and seven community colleges. Reciprocal borrowing privileges for faculty and students will exist at all of these institutions.

The first CJCLS Program Development Award was given to Chemeketa Community College LRC's Cooperative Collection Development Committee. This committee participates in a consortium of public and academic libraries in Oregon's mid–Willamette Valley. Under a grant from the Fred Meyer Charitable Trust, a number of the libraries began utilizing a shared on-line catalog, E-mail, and daily courier service for cooperative collection assessment and development. Chemeketa librarians, currently the only community college participants, hope eventually the system will include the LRCs of all thirteen of Oregon's two-year colleges.

Mandated completion testing and increased efforts to help community college transfers succeed will create a need for articulation agreements and sequential levels of bibliographic instruction between two- and four-year colleges. Librarians at Clinton Community College, Plattsburgh, New York, and SUNY/Plattsburgh are successfully carrying out such an agreement.

Community College LRC Networking
State-wide community college library networks are emerging in Florida, Maryland, Ohio, and Washington. Florida's College Center for Library Automation will serve the sixty-four libraries in the state's twenty-eight community colleges.

The system will have a data base of 2.5 million records and utilize an existing telecommunications network (FIRN). Users will also have access to the 6 million-record system developed five years ago for the state's nine four-year institutions and to a variety of on-line periodicals indexes, such as Wilsondisc and InfoTrac. The system will feature term searching and will provide off-campus access.

LRC Legislative Involvement

In 1985 California's community college librarians—with assistance from the state library—received an LSCA demonstration grant to establish a position in the state chancellor's office for a community college library/LRC administrator which would parallel those existing for the state's two groups of four-year institutions. The LRC administrator used the grant to hire a consultant to develop special output measures and—after documenting significant underfunding of the state's two-year college LRCs—acquired $8 million in state funds, the first in a series of "catch-up" appropriations. Under the subsequent 1987 Community College Reform Bill, LRCs will begin to receive program-based, rather than attendance-based, funding.

The assistant dean of instructional resources/library director at Harrisburg Area Community College was instrumental in getting an HEA Title II-D grant for his region's eighteen-member college-library consortium to create a CD-ROM union catalog of over 2 million records, which members utilize for interlibrary loans and reciprocal borrowing. He has also been actively involved in lobbying efforts of the Pennsylvania Library Association to get a $20 million appropriation for technology and collection development and preservation for the state's academic libraries and has been elected to represent those libraries as a delegate to the Pennsylvania Governor's Conference on Libraries.

Indeed, as the combined pressures of accountability, funding patterns, and new technology have increasingly merged the identity of the community college LRC with that of other libraries, many of its professionals participated in the recent White House Conference on Libraries. In that capacity they served as proud representatives of institutions and programs which have long demonstrated dedication and commitment to the three conference themes: productivity, literacy, and democracy.

Works Cited

Anderson, Susan. "Shared Libraries: Focus on Florida." *Community and Junior College Libraries* Jan. 1990:3–16.

Ducote, Richard L., Alicia T. Tibbals, and Steven E. Prouty. "Active Learning and the LRC." In *The Role of the Learning Resources Center in Instruction.* New Directions for Community Colleges, 71. San Francisco: Jossey-Bass, 1990. 63–70.

Major, Howard. "LRC-Based Professional Development." In *The Role of the Learning Resources Center in Instruction.* New Directions for Community Colleges, 71. San Francisco: Jossey-Bass, 1990. 39–43.

U.S. Department of Education. Office of Educational Research and Improvement. National Center for Education Statistics. *Digest of Education Statistics 1989.* 25th ed. Washington: GPO, 1989.

FUTURES: THE CONTINUED SEARCH
FOR EXCELLENCE

Camila A. Alire and Alice Beverley Gass

As professionals, we look to the present and past to display our accomplishments in community college learning resources programs and to plan for the future. What does the future hold for community college learning resource programs, and how must the learning resources concept be altered to meet it? What do the practitioners and leaders in the field think about the future? What are they doing to prepare for the years ahead that might be valuable for others to consider?

This chapter attempts to answer these and other concerns about the future of learning resources programs. This chapter also addresses library automation. What is being done and what does the future hold for the automating of library services?

A Problematic Concept?

There has been much to celebrate in the development period of the community college learning resources program. Qualitative terms such as *creativity, flexibility, innovation* are but a few that have been used to describe the learning resources model of delivery of library, audiovisual, telecommunications, and instructional services. But there are now a number of doubts residing in its present about what *learning resources* is and what it may become in the future. There have been voices raised expressing concern about the viability of the learning resources program concept in the community college.

Gloria Terwilliger of Northern Virginia Community College mentioned as early as 1982 that learning resources programs were diminishing in their energy; "a modicum of inertia has been created" (1).

Lee Hisle of Austin Community College in Texas expressed a similar note of pessimism in his description of the learning resources concept as one that allowed programs to be included that did not seem to fit anywhere else in the college but did fit the philosophy of "anything to support instruction." Hisle clearly implied that the learning resources program concept is diffused and devoid of clear goals and direction ("Libraries in Learning Resources" 379).

Even more recently than Terwilliger and Hisle, Doris Cruger Dale, a learning resources observer, found that the library/learning resources program image is not projected in college catalogs. Dale suggested that this lack raises real questions about whether the library is fulfilling its teaching function in the community college (233–234).

Charges such as lacking in momentum, being devoid of clear goals, and having no impact in its environment are but three we identified in the literature. We wondered if there were other issues and concerns for the future of learning resources in the community college besides these. If there were, what were they, and what could be done about them? We decided to examine the literature even more closely and solicit the opinions of a number of professionals in the field in an attempt to identify some of the more problematic issues facing community college learning resources; to assess program viability and resilience; and to determine if we could offer any worthwhile suggestions for their future.

Because learning resources programs are structured and organized so differently from college to college, we decided it would be helpful to focus on three common elements: administration, staffing, and the relationship to teaching and learning.

Administration: Passive or Proactive?

It is our opinion that successful learning resources programs will exhibit similar characteristics. These characteristics may be determined by gathering responses to the following questions: How is the learning resources program viewed by the president, the chief academic officer of the college, and/or other politically influential college individuals? How effective is the learning resources administrator in providing leadership in shaping or creating this view? And, how responsive is the program to the instructional needs of the college?

There should be many community colleges where the learning resources directors have been successful in combining these characteristics in ways which might serve as models for establishing new or changing existing programs. Awareness of these models could help in renewing our sense of purpose and reviving our lagging spirits about what we do every day.

Instructional Leadership

The effective director recognizes that the learning resources program is successful when it is a reflection of its parent college. The philosophical basis of the community college movement is in serving the needs of the community and, to be successful, designing and conducting instructional programs to fit those community needs. So it is with learning resources programs. Where a program is linked to the needs of the college, success follows.

Having once received educational services precisely designed for their college, college administrators value or learn to value the program and its services. Consequently, the director has increasing room and opportunity to create the kind of learning resources program that is most appropriate for his or her college. The more success the director experiences in developing a program, the more opportunity there is for continuing success.

When we interviewed John Thomas of Davidson County Community College in North Carolina, he described his role within the college administration as being one where he spoke with a "voice equal with other college leaders" (1989). In fact, Thomas believed that the learning resources program was a partner in the instructional processes of the college equal to all other organizational units and was perceived by the rest of the college in this light as he accepted and assumed his position as an academic leader. He suggested, somewhat wryly, that we (LRC directors, librarians, and staff) do not

have a "divine right to respect." Even though we may believe
passionately in the value of our services to instruction, we will
be effective leaders of learning resources programs by tem-
pering that passion with efforts to gain the respect and confidence from our colleagues and to participate responsibly in
decision making for the college. We must believe in and
support the mission of the college first before we can shape
the mission of learning resources programs successfully. It
would be fair to say that Thomas believed that the success of
these programs is directly tied to our willingness to be committed first to the success of the college.

Ralph Steinke, Dean of Learning Resources at DeAnza
College in California, expressed his view of supporting the
college mission. Steinke's thoughts paralleled those of John
Thomas:

> All too often learning resources people are not part of
> the decision-making process. Once they get into top
> level management, they are forced to get the bigger
> picture—it provides views of how all these things [pro-
> grams within the college] tie together. [1990]

Steinke advised learning resources personnel to determine
what the "influential persona" of the college are interested in,
and to find ways in which our learning resources programs can
fit into those ideas. "Once an LRC director has identified those
areas of interest and ascertained the local political climate, s/he
can better formulate a strategy to increase the clout of the LRC"
("Learning Resources Personalities" 33).

Planning

Once we have determined what our users want from our
programs, then we must decide how best to meet those needs
if we want to contribute significantly to our colleges' instructional programs. We must engage in strategic planning for the
delivery of effective learning resources programs and services. The value of planning does seem to have achieved a high
level of acceptance within the community college. Likewise,
the idea of planning has permeated learning resources programs and again will usually be a mirror image of college-wide
planning efforts.

If the *Standards for Two-Year College Learning Resources*

Programs, especially the first one which states that "the college shall develop a comprehensive statement of the mission of the learning resources program based on the nature and purposes of the institution" ("Standards" 758), have any validity, then we should find that most learning resources programs will have mission statements to guide planning activities and daily operations. If that is the case, then an examination of these mission statements would provide an interesting view of the learning resources movement nationally.

Funding and the Future

Susan Martin struck a particularly resonant chord when she said that one of the benefits of planning would be in knowing what funds are needed. Funding, indeed, is an issue which rides into our futures, hanging as tightly as it can, onto our horses. Let's face it, funding has long been, and ever shall be, problematic. We will do well to find ways to make funding a reality of which we are masters. We must accept the notion that when it comes to funding our college programs, "the library is everyone's second priority" (Martin 400).

Second priority or not, learning resources program administrators will find that they must keep funding and fundraising as their first priority in the future. Heretofore, we have principally looked to internal institutional funding mechanisms as the sole source of operational funds. This will have to change in the future as fiscal problems will mean that "planning and resource development will be the difference between vitality and excellence in contrast to survival and maintenance" (Bender 6).

Gretchen Neill of DeKalb College in Georgia reported that, although she felt good about the amount of her college's budget which is allocated to the learning resources program as compared with the rest of the college, these resources do not go far enough. "The bottom line [for the LRC] looks huge," but learning resources programs in multi-campus colleges are expensive. Neill noted that the cost of serials, the provision of recreational materials which duplicate public library collections, the high volume of intracampus and interlibrary lending are costly ventures which have been or may be the focus of philosophical repositioning in the future of DeKalb College's learning resources program (1989).

On a similar note, Tobin Clark of San Joaquin Delta Community College in California anticipated more stable funding for community colleges and learning resources programs especially now that there were mechanisms in place in California to shift from local to state funding for community colleges. She thought the future looked somewhat brighter because of that (1990).

Obviously, funding is a volatile and state-by-state matter. Whatever the status of funding and budgeting may be around the country, one thing is certain: funding will continually be a source of concern and will always demand our time as local and state economies fluctuate. Creating a new perspective toward the value, and even necessity, of fund-raising is clearly indicated for the future of learning resources programs.

Committees and Friends Group

In addition to fund-raising, the learning resource program administrators also need to consider the role of advisory committees. These committees are a typical organizational support mechanism in the community colleges which has worked more or less effectively for instructional programs. Their degree of effectiveness varies with each college and will probably work to the same degree of effectiveness for the learning resources program as for the parent college. It is a mechanism which we may or may not decide to put to work in support of our programs, primarily as we find it working at our colleges.

If advisory committees are really instructional "power brokers" at your college, then by all means organize one for assistance in guiding and politicizing your program for the future. Include representatives from all constituencies: students, faculty, and community. Use them to your best advantage—as power brokers, fund raisers, advisors, program designers. There will definitely be advantages to having such a group advising you and supporting the learning resources program. Whatever works at your college is the point. If there is some type of advisory committee structure working well for other instructional programs on campus, then imitate! If it's best to organize a Friends group as part of the college foundation, then consider it!

On the other hand, we recognize that these committees

may be absolutely without impact on your campus and have no value. At Collin County Community College in Texas, Richard DuCote saw no reason for having one of these committees. He thought that it was a model left over from the university environment and without merit for his program. DuCote and his staff found it better to build their constituencies through a process which he referred to as integrating self and staff into the institution through participation on committees and task forces. "That's where the best opportunity to have an impact comes" (DuCote 1989).

However we do decide to chart out courses administratively for the future, such matters as leadership, funding, planning, and advisory committees are but a few of the things which will demand special consideration whether we like it or not. There are any number of other administrative issues which will need attention and adjustment which may be as critical as these.

Staffing: Our Silent Majority

In the area of staffing, we have identified several key issues which would appear on any list as demanding our energies in the future. Issues here, also, will be more or less critical depending on the local climate.

Staff Development

Probably the one issue that comes to mind first is staff development. This is, and will be for some time to come, a critical staffing issue because the personnel or human resources components of learning resources programs are, without question, their most valuable and important assets. This value is partially derived, of course, from the vast tangible fiscal assets required to employ qualified staffs.

If we are to meet the future with any sense of responsibility, then we will be forced to evaluate the training and development needs that exist for those human resources—professional, clerical, paraprofessional, and technical—who operate our programs. Staff development is necessary to upgrade skills, to revitalize and reenergize staff, and to preserve and protect human capital.

One of the best reasons for attending increasingly to staff development was that given by Ralph Steinke. He credited the staff of learning resources programs with making the difference between adequate and excellent learning resources programs. Steinke recognized how important the staff was in leading and making change happen (1990). Staff development provides them with growth opportunities and preparation for leadership.

Another reason that staff development will grow in importance is that typically many of our staff members have been in the same positions for several years and need an opportunity for rejuvenation and skills enhancement if we want them to continue to contribute meaningfully to our programs. Since we all will not be able, or even want, to attend national conferences or expensive workshops, we must provide staff development opportunities within our colleges and within our learning resources facilities.

To be meaningful, we believe that staff development programs must be designed to meet the needs of the individual staff members. Again, a needs assessment process for determining the most suitable kinds of staff development opportunities is essential at the local level or even the statewide level. The value of needs assessment for staff development planning and programming was regarded as basic at the School of Library and Information Science at North Carolina Central University, which had offered tailor-made staff development programs for libraries and librarians in that state at minimal cost. Through its unique program, the library school has employed a librarian/faculty member who actually consults with librarians across the state to identify staff development needs. He then develops and implements programs out in the field to meet those specific needs.

In the summer of 1989, for example, the library school assisted in the implementation of a legal reference workshop for community college librarians who work in colleges with paralegal and criminal justice programs throughout the state. Workshop participants expressed overwhelming satisfaction with a program so specifically designed with their needs in mind. It was so successful that, in the fall of 1990, they presented an advanced legal reference workshop once again targeted especially at community college librarians.

Diversity

Diversity of student population is another issue which is gathering momentum for many learning resources programs. Community college learning resources program administrators need to prepare their staffs to deal with the need to recognize, accept, and assist a student body that is diverse in gender, ethnicity, race, age, and physical ability.

At DeKalb College, one of the greatest staff development needs will be for programs that address cultural diversity. As DeKalb and many other colleges become increasingly populated by international and multi-cultural students, it will be necessary to prepare staff members to communicate with and appreciate these diverse groups (Neill 1989).

Interestingly and coincidentally, DuCote used the word diversity in describing a quality which he believed characterized the staff he wanted to attract to Collin Community College's emerging learning resources program. He wanted a staff that represents diversity of experiences, cultural backgrounds skills and, most of all, points of view. When interviewing potential staff members, he and his staff look especially for individuals with mind-sets different from the "DuCote" mind-set. "Hire as many different ones as you can. With diversity comes freshness and new ideas." DuCote also believed that staff development opportunities should be available to "give individuals the opportunity to change" (1989).

Change Management

Change management is unquestionably another issue revving up for the future of learning resources programs. Unless we find ways to assist our staffs in meeting inevitable and ubiquitous change, then facing the future really will be rough.

The most difficult part of implementing any new program or idea is dealing with the Saran-wrap of fear that seems to serve as protection against anything that is new or different. Once a new thing enters our environs, this protective packaging seems to grab hold and cling to some staff members, rendering them nearly powerless to deal with that which is new. Managers responsive to the needs of the staff will anticipate this potential problem and will work feverishly to make change as easy as possible.

Another change to be managed is that brought about by time and shifts in work loads. Tobin Clark reported that one of the weightiest matters facing the learning resources program at her college had to do with the designing of a new organizational structure for the future. This had become necessary to accommodate changes brought to learning resources by such factors as technological developments, a large number of retirements, jobs overstuffed with duties and responsibilities, and a future shortage of qualified staff. Clark anticipated bringing in a consultant to review the staffing situation and advise them accordingly (1990).

Technical services staff, especially, will continue to experience this kind of change as automation and technology alter work patterns significantly. It may be that staff in these areas will need to be retrained for assuming more responsibility in public service areas of the library and in finding the means to use technical and paraprofessionals more effectively.

Support staff should be given responsibility for tasks which they are qualified to handle, thus lessening the burden on professional staff. In technical services, copy cataloging needs to be handed over to the technicians. At reference and information desks, technicians and paraprofessionals can be trained to be the front-line responders handling the repetitive and directional questions. In the computer center, technical-level personnel can maintain equipment and introduce the beginners to technology and software. Audiovisual and telecommunications departments have always valued technicians and paraprofessionals. Skills labs, too, can make much use of technical-level staff. Technicians and technical-level training are essential to the community college ethic and play a vital part in staffing learning resources programs.

Professional Viability

If we make appropriate use of technicians and paraprofessionals, then learning resources faculty and professional staff will have the opportunity to be just that—professional. They should be instructional leaders for the college, aggressive marketers, skilled negotiators in the budget process, political dynamos in their environments, experts in their fields, and proactive, involved members in professional, trade, and community college associations.

One of the ways that we can enhance our images within the college and within the community college movement is by playing a more active and visible role in community college–related organizations. The newly formed National Council for Learning Resources of the American Association of Community and Junior Colleges (AACJC) is a viable forum.

Unless we are aware of and involved in matters surrounding community colleges, then matters that are particularly learning resources–related will gain little attention or credibility at the national level. All community college personnel need an awareness of the issues facing our programs at the national level. Until there is a general community college–wide interest in learning resources programs and services, then we will continue to be rather invisible and seemingly unimportant. We need increased visibility and acceptance by our colleagues to enable us to work for students and instructors in the truly meaningful ways that we know are possible.

Staff development, new patterns of organization, diversity concerns, and management for change are all issues looming large in our futures. The actual shape which each of these assumes will vary from college to college and state to state, but each will require creativity and tenacity in the search for the best solutions.

Teaching and Learning: The Buck Stops Here

Issues of administering and staffing learning resource programs are important only insofar as they are addressed against the background of the real reason for our being—the teaching and learning processes that occur within our colleges. All our concerns about managing change and retraining staff and budgeting are meaningless if we are unable to retain our vision of what we can do for instruction and our perspective about why we do it. If that is so, what are some of the really critical issues facing us in the next several years for teaching and learning in the community college?

Information Literacy
The literature suggests that community college libraries or learning resources programs can take a more active role in

supporting and promoting the excellence of their colleges through more effective instructional programs. We need to make certain that we are doing everything we can to ensure that our students are information literate.

We must design programs to teach students how to find and use information. Students use the library to find information now in a manner referred to as "bitting." They want to find the smallest amount of information in the least time. Consequently, the analytical processes are bypassed.

We must resist the urge to "reduce knowledge to predigested information to be retrieved by prearranged procedures" (Ray 150). Perhaps the real value of CD-ROM-based reference tools is in freeing the students from the laborious and procedural tasks of identifying sources. CD-ROM speeds up the searching process. It gives students more time and opportunity to use their evaluative skills to determine relevance and accuracy of information and to develop and use their critical-thinking skills to produce more thoughtful analyses of their findings.

One of the most vital issues confronting learning resources programs in the arena of information literacy is the need for bibliographic instruction to be more carefully planned and executed to ensure that tomorrow's students are prepared to survive in the changing and competitive work force. At a symposium sponsored by Columbia University and the University of Colorado in March 1987, the role of libraries in the pursuit of academic excellence served as the focus of discussion among leaders from both the higher education community and academic librarianship (Brandehoff 443–445; Breivik 44–52).

E. Gordon Gee and Patricia Breivik defined a good learning experience as one that "imitates reality . . . is active not passive . . . is individualized . . . makes provision for a variety of learning styles . . . is up-to-date . . . and [recognizes] that students learn best when the environment is least threatening" (Gee and Breivik 34–36).

This advice is especially appropriate for those of us designing bibliographic instruction (BI) programs. We need to give careful consideration to this definition and search for ways to bring these qualities to life in BI programs. It is equally important that we find ways to assist faculty in bringing these qualities to the design of BI, especially by advocating that course-related library instruction is an effective method of bringing relevance and action to any learning experiences which they are creating.

Developmental Students and Learning Resources

Colette A. Wagner and Augusta S. Kappner suggested that if the library is to participate fully in the successful learning experiences of non-traditional students, new techniques of bibliographic instruction must be developed. Librarians should be "empowered within the context of their respective institutions to participate more fully in the instructional process" (Wagner and Kappner 55).

In the area of service to developmental students, we must refocus our attention and find ways to meet their special needs. Cecilia Suarez related her experience at Miami-Dade Community College in developing a cooperative and innovative program of support by the college library for the developmental or compensatory education programs there (487–499).

At Davidson Community College, the learning resources program has been expanded to include the provision of non-traditional instructional literacy programs such as GED, adult high school, and adult basic education. A pressing need there is to find appropriate means to deliver services to these developmental students. What Davidson County Community College and others finally do to assimilate these students into traditional instructional programs and how they provide for their special learning needs could serve as a useful example for us all (Thomas 1989). We also think more programs like the one presented by the Community and Junior College Library Section at the 1989 ALA Conference in Dallas— "Responding to the Needs of Developmental Students"— will be increasingly important in the future.

Instructional Design and Development

One challenge that has faced us since the inception of the learning resources concept has been the need for faculty to understand what we can offer in the design and delivery of instruction. At DeKalb College, Gretchen Neill reported that in the fall of 1989, new faculty requested that workshops be available for them on instructional design. This was the first time in years that faculty had initiated such a request. Neill used the term "neutral territory" to characterize why she thought faculty saw the learning resources center as being a safe place to go to receive assistance in revising and upgrading their instruction. Willingness to admit that one's work needs revision and the courage to begin to change will require "neutral and safe" places (Neill 1989).

This idea of the neutrality of learning resources services and staff cropped up in our discussion with DuCote also. We will do well to assist teaching faculty in understanding the neutrality of our environment so that they can really use our services to their best advantage.

Collin County Community College's Learning Resources Center (LRC) is also deeply involved in instructional design and delivery. Since nearly all courses there have a required lab component, there are a number of learning and skills labs scattered throughout the college. Because the lab administered by learning resources is cross-disciplinary and open to any student at the college, there has been the opportunity for the learning resources lab to achieve a viability for the entire college's instructional efforts that other labs are not able to attain because of their more narrowly defined focus.

Likewise, the learning resources program at Collin County has within it another cross-disciplinary tool for the delivery of instruction: an earth station capable of receiving and transmitting satellite signals. DuCote believes that we must be in the forefront with such new techniques and methods of instructional delivery. Finding the means to stay on the cutting edge of instruction and incorporating technology in its delivery is, and will be, a major responsibility of learning resources programs (DuCote 1989).

Library Automation: Plugs and Connections

One of the best attributes of a community college is the flexibility of its internal structure, which encourages creativity and innovation. The community college learning resources program is equally innovative when dealing with library automation. Many community college learning resources programs have marched right along with their four-year counter-parts in implementing various automation functions in their library services component. This section of the chapter addresses the impact of library automation in various community college learning resource programs throughout the United States.

Of the many community college library programs that have some type of automation in place, those programs selected to be included in this section of the chapter represent colleges from various geographical regions in the county. We tried to include a variety of programs, such as multi-campus library programs, state community college system programs, programs with branches, and library programs in multi-type library consortia. Some of these library programs were using various types of library automation, such as compact disc technology, computer-assisted retrieval, and on-line public-access catalogs.

We recognized that there are many community college library programs which have minimal or no library automation in place. This is understandable given the budget situations on campuses. However, we wanted to present community college library automation in terms of the changes that have taken place as well as what the future could be for those not yet at the automation stage. We are sure that as we write about the future of library automation, it is probably happening already at some community college library. More power to you folks!

The learning resources personnel interviewed for the automation portion of this chapter were willing to share what they accomplished with their colleagues throughout the community college world. David Butler, Associate Dean at the Chabot Community College's Learning Resources Center in Hayward, California, represented LRCs from a multi-campus point of view. Another multi-campus point of view came from Lee Hisle, District Director of Learning Resources Services for Austin Community College's multi-campus district in Austin, Texas. Hisle works with three head librarians from three main campuses along with head librarians for extension services and technical services. Maricopa County Community College District in Arizona was the largest multi-campus system (ten campuses) included in this work. Laurita Moore de Diaz, Director of Library and Information Services Technologies, District Office, shared Maricopa's perspectives on library automation with us. Florida's Hillsborough Community College's four-campus library system was represented by Viveca Yoshikawa, Library Automation Specialist, from the Tampa campus.

Although Portland (Oregon) Community College is a multi-campus system, Barbara Swanson, Director of Learning Resources Center in Portland, reported that their networking as a member of North Valley Link is vital to their automating efforts. In that same vein, Illinois Central College, which includes a main and two branch libraries, relied exclusively on a multi-type library consortium, RSA (Resource Sharing Alliance of West Central Illinois), for all its automation efforts. To give an idea of RSA's membership size, it includes four of Illinois's library systems. Bill Lindgren, Director of the Learning Resources Center at Illinois Central College, shared his views with us.

What is done in Colorado was different from all the other examples included in this work. The majority of the Colorado community colleges are under a state system, the Colorado Community Colleges and Occupational Education System (CCCOES). CC LINK is the consortium of CCCOES libraries formed specifically to automate using one system. CC LINK includes the largest community colleges as well as the smallest in the state. Pikes Peak Community College in Colorado Springs represented CC LINK in this chapter.

Also included in the interviews was Charlet Key, Library Director, Blackhawk College, Moline, Illinois. Blackhawk is a good example of a library which did not have an automated integrated library system but had some library functions automated and was working diligently to network with its multi-type/bi-state consortium, Quad Link, and other state networks to provide automated services to Blackhawk College students and faculty.

In many cases, fiscal constraints prohibited community college learning resources directors from maintaining the state-of-the-art status. Because of this, we were equally impressed by the willingness to look at networking to achieve or continue their library automation goals. CC LINK and RSA are good examples of this.

Automation will continue to change, and community college libraries will be expected to stay abreast of these changes. With continual software and hardware technological upgrades, enhancements, and complete modifications, the only constant in library automation is its continual state of flux.

Automating Library Functions: Revolution or Evolution?

Joseph Rosenthal, University Librarian at University of California–Berkeley, believed that changes in library operations and services were evolutionary because they incorporated extensions and modifications of what was already done instead of implementing new services (Riggs and Sabine 6). Automating library functions at the community college level is also more evolutionary than revolutionary. For example, libraries started using a commercial vendor to automate one particular function, such as circulation; or they developed an in-house on-line public-access catalog (OPAC) for use. In most cases, the evolution to an automated integrated library system soon followed.

It appeared, at least with the community college libraries we polled, that the main emphasis in library automation was to incorporate an OPAC. OPACs allow the user to access the library's material holdings using a computer terminal. The bibliographic entry can be accessed using keyword/Boolean searching. The manual use of a traditional card catalog will be a thing of the past.

The OPAC seemed to be one of the most widespread library automation functions desired or implemented at the community college level. In most cases, the community college libraries selected commercial systems that allowed for integration of other library functions. The advantage of a commercial system is that most upgrades developed by the vendor are available to the customer.

In-house enhancements to a commercially produced OPAC are becoming more common. Pikes Peak Community College Learning Resources Center, one of the Colorado CC LINK consortium members using the CARL (Colorado Alliance of Research Libraries) library system, has enhanced its OPAC offerings for students, faculty, and the community. "The library's OPAC includes a college calendar of events, the LRC Directory of functions and locations, a list of topographical maps, and a list of telephone directories available" (Armintor 1990).

Maricopa Community College District's in-house enhancement to the ATLAS software produced by DRA (Data Research Associates) was a dial-up phone directory. Laurita Moore de Diaz stated, "Future in-house enhancements for Maricopa's multi-campus OPACs available in a demonstration program include governing board minutes, district-wide job announcements, and job descriptions" (1989).

Creativity is not stifled when using a commercial product. The best analogy to use here is Hewlett-Packard's "What if . . . ?" television commercials. There is no doubt in our minds that a few "What if . . . ?"s or "Why couldn't we . . . ?"s ignited an idea into a reality. One must remember using a commercial vendor to automate a library does not negate the possibilities of pursuing future in-house enhancements of that automated library system.

What about cooperative efforts between vendors who are jointly designing ways to provide enhanced services to the user? CARL in Colorado and DRA's ATLAS System have been individually working with Information Access Company (IAC). Colorado CC LINK and Maricopa County Community College District library users are benefitting from such cooperation. For example, CARL and IAC cooperated in a project to put two IAC data bases on-line on the CARL system, which allows users to search these data bases through a CARL terminal. In addition, the users are able to order full-text microfilmed IAC articles "to be delivered either online to the screen or offline through telefacsimile" ("ON TRACK" 9). Maricopa, on the other hand, bought a particular data base from IAC and the license for a DRA programming software that allows them to use IAC on their DRA system (Moore de Diaz 1989).

Integrated Library Systems

More community college library programs using a commercially produced, automated OPAC have an integrated system. Such a system allows for various library functions to be integrated using that one system. For example, most OPACs are integrated with a circulation module. Portland Community College (Swanson 1989) and Austin Community College

(Hisle 1989) both used the DYNIX system, which integrated the OPAC with their circulation function. DYNIX also integrated an electronic mail function that is used by both college libraries to communicate with their other campus libraries.

Hillsborough Community College in Florida utilized the Columbia Library System (formerly OCELOT) for its four campus libraries which included OPAC and circulation functions (Yoshikawa 1989).

The CARL system implemented by Colorado CC LINK consortium provides integration capabilities with its OPAC, circulation, serials, and other modules and is revising its acquisitions module. The use of these integrated modules varies among the CC LINK members depending on the level of sophistication of each library's functions. Some CC LINK members were just trying to get their records into MARC format while other members have been using the MARC format for years.

As previously mentioned, almost all of the community college libraries included had some type of integrated system. Blackhawk Community College did not have an OPAC, but their circulation function had been automated using CLSI software. There was a Quad Link Consortium subcommittee investigating the possibility of an OPAC on compact disc to be used within the consortium. Blackhawk saw its automation future in the scope of its consortium membership as well as linking up to other state networks (Key 1989). The willingness to network with others to provide services to their individual community college campuses is one of the prevailing themes that appears throughout this section.

One of the pioneer library functions in automation was that of cataloging. Using OCLC has become a mainstay in automation. Ironically, for many community college libraries in the country, automating their cataloging function would be the "future" for them. These libraries still do not have their records in MARC format; other libraries have integrated systems which can download the OCLC tapes onto their commercial system data base. Moore de Diaz reported that the Maricopa County Community College District was able to do OCLC copy cataloging as well as original cataloging on DRA's ATLAS system.

Most of the libraries reported that the serials and acquisitions functions were not within their integrated system. DRA's ATLAS system at Maricopa did provide serial and acquisition modules, as did CARL for the Colorado CC LINK libraries. Hillsborough Community College was investigating a serials module available through Columbia Library System according to Yoshikawa.

Swanson at Portland Community College reported the capability of downloading their bibliographic record from OCLC onto their DYNIX acquisition subsystem. Some libraries enlisted the automation features provided by various book vendors. Other libraries used various commercial programming software to assist them in automating some of their acquisitions functions. Pikes Peak Community College library used the college's minicomputer and software. Austin Community College used the OCLC acquisition subsystem to meet their acquisition needs. "We also use SuperCALC to determine the allocation formula for our various subject disciplines budgets" (Hisle 1989).

"For serials automation, Portland Community College uses the data base system REFLEX to keep track of our accounts, renewals, and destination of serials to the various campuses" (Swanson 1989). Illinois Central College through the RSA consortium was just starting a project to use the RSA data base for serials. Illinois's SILO (Serials in Illinois On-line) project has many academic and public libraries' serial titles and holdings on-line. "RSA staff had taken the holdings of RSA members only from the SILO data base and entered it into RSA's data base bank and made that serial information available to RSA users" (Lindgren 1989). Coupling ingenuity with resource-sharing efforts, Illinois Central College students and faculty have access to information far beyond their campus. Lindgren also reported that Illinois Central will be able to provide access to ILLINET ON-LINE, a network of academic libraries, in the near future through the RSA consortium, using UTLAS/Series 50 integrated library system software.

Networking

Illinois Central College's example of resource sharing via networking is a good one. Another example is the networking at Blackhawk College. *Access* and *resource sharing* are words that link Blackhawk College Library to its future in library automation. ILLINET ON-LINE (IO) provided "nodes" to other libraries to access IO's data base using a local telephone number, thus eliminating prohibitive long distance telephone charges. Although Blackhawk College students and faculty did not have an OPAC with their local holdings, they did have immediate access to a large data base of holdings throughout the state (Key 1989). Again, this was a prime example of how some community college libraries were able to network with others to provide maximum service to their students and faculty.

In a sense, the grandfather of networking is interlibrary loan (ILL). Because of the users' ability to access information more readily, the ILL function has become increasingly important. Again, the use of OCLC has been the mainstay in this area of automation. All but Maricopa's ILL functions were separate from the integrated system in place. However, ILL telefacsimile machines were in place in all but one community college library interviewed. This automation function is extremely important when working in a multi-campus environment. What does the future hold for ILL? For those libraries with integrated systems, the future may include an upgrade that incorporates the ILL function as part of the integrated system. More specifically, the future could have a user-driven ILL function which would allow the student to complete the ILL transaction at the OPAC terminal.

Illinois Central College (ICC) already has implemented this type of user-driven function through the RSA consortium. At the OPAC, the student finds a bibliographic entry for a book that ICC does not own. The student needs only to press a key, and the search will continue to the other libraries to locate the book. The programming logic is based on searching libraries with closest geographical proximity first rather than on an alphabetical listing of libraries in the state.

Once the book is located, the student just presses the "print" key and receives a complete screen printout with the bibliographic data on the book and the name of the lending library. The student then takes the printout to the ILL office where the ILL transaction is sent immediately (Lindgren 1989). This service is coupled with a daily courier service.

User Services

The most interesting of all areas of library automation was the area of reference services. It appeared that this was the service area which allowed for the most creativity. We were pleased to discover that all the libraries included had some reference service/sources automated. Computer-assisted research was provided. Various CD-ROM products were in use, such as encyclopedias and indexes.

There was strong sentiment that CD technology was best suited to the community college library. "CD-ROM technology needs not only to give the citation but the hard copy [full text] immediately via a printer attached to the terminal" (Butler 1989). The future would include CD workstations where students could access all the CD software through a "jukebox" system. This would allow the student to switch from function to function without physically moving from the workstation.

The use of a hypertext system would allow students to go from one information piece to many others, at their own pace, choosing their information paths, and "gathering individually relevant information with ultimate efficiency" (Keough 60). Software programming systems have been produced as tools for hypertext. Such a software system could also act as the "access gate" to sources of information contained in various types of media. This would allow the ability to control external devices, such as CD-ROM and interactive video (Ragan 39). More specifically, a hypertext software programming system would allow the programmer to create applications using text, graphics, sound, and video, and combine them into one program.

The best example of this application is CD–Interactive Video (CD-IV), which is a multi-media system that joins together video, audio, text, software storage, and retrieval process. Viveca Yoshikawa shared her thoughts on the future relating to CD-ROM activities:

> Imagine a student at a CD-IV workstation working on a term paper reading the encyclopedia text on a screen. The student then reviews a short video with sound on the topic and uses the periodical index available on disc to locate citations on the topic with full text provided.

> From there the student, using the word processor at-
> tached to the workstation, types and prints out his term
> paper. [1989]

That is the future for students in a community college library!
Also, using a software programming system such as Hyper-
Card, for example, library tours could be automated, saving
staff time to provide other more needed reference services.

A less labor-intensive basic bibliographic instruction could
be offered utilizing a system like HyperCard. HyperCard,
like other hypertext software programming systems, is a "visual information center" that provides screens of information
called cards. The cards have buttons or icons that perform
special functions, "such as revealing more information, linking to other screens, or providing user feedback" (Ragan 38).
Ultimately, in a finished product, there are "stacks" of cards
that allow the users to access information at their own pace
and also retrieve the information discriminately.

Once the hypertext BI program is in place, students could
proceed through a well-designed BI stack that can even encourage interaction by setting up a dialogue with the system.
If a student only wants to know how to use OPAC or the card
catalog, he/she can enter at any point in the stack to that
section without going through the entire BI presentation.
This is the future of community college library services.

We have alluded to future scenarios concerning library
automation throughout this section. For those libraries which
have an integrated system but do not belong to some type of
network or consortium, the future could be to network with
other library systems in their state and provide their students
and faculties access to the holdings of many other libraries.

For those community college library programs with integrated library systems in a consortium, their future may be
additional automated functions added to their integrated system or additional in-house enhancements for their own students and faculties. For all of those with integrated library
systems, the future could include linking their system to their
colleges' minicomputer for intracampus access.

For students and faculty who have microcomputers, mo-
dems, and the other necessary peripheral equipment at home,
their future may allow them to access interactive learning

materials provided in the library or to dial-in for electronic reference services. Moore de Diaz stated:

> Activated/accelerated learning would be at its best. Students would be able to use the library's advanced workstation, which would allow simultaneous audio, video, and data communication and multi-tasking with a multitude of systems and services. Students would have control of their learning processes according to their learning styles. [1989]

David Butler from Chabot Community College agreed.

> The LRC will become more proactive in the teaching/ learning process. It will become a major information distribution center for distance learning as well as for learning on campus. [1989]

The creative juices are flowing in community college library programs throughout the country. This is what we are all about. Library automation need not start or end with an on-line public-access catalog. Library automation will play a key role in the future of library services.

Conclusion

We had hoped to conclude brilliantly and passionately about the future of learning resources programs. Instead, we discovered that it is the daily operational journey through these programs that finally determines our future. We evolve into the future just as Joseph Rosenthal said earlier about the evolution of library services. There really is little that is revolutionary about it. The sense of drama and dynamism about the future is better conceived as we perceive it retrospectively. This does not, however, lessen our enthusiasm about the future of these learning resources programs.

All the systems we develop or install, whether on-line catalogs or interactive video learning stations, will be there for one purpose, and one purpose only: to enhance and facilitate the teaching/learning processes that are at the center of our colleges.

Maybe a useful challenge for us is not to revitalize the idea of the learning resources program as the heart of the college but to be instrumental in helping to put the heart back into teaching and learning. There is much to look forward to in our future, especially as we envision and create a future where we keep the role and contribution of learning resources programs focused sharply on instruction.

We in learning resources are part of that future and, at the same time, preparing for it. We encourage learning resources personnel to continue to be visonary, creative, innovative, and flexible in supporting the instructional process at their community colleges.

Works Cited

Armintor, Bob. Telephone interview. 12 January 1990.

Bender, Louis W. "Fund Raising to Assure College Library Vitality." *Community College Review* 17.1 (1989): 5–10.

Brandehoff, Susan. "A Meeting of Minds." *American Libraries* 18 (1987): 443–445.

Breivik, Patricia S. "Making the Most of Libraries in the Search for Academic Excellence." *Change* 19.4 (1987): 44–52.

Butler, David. Telephone interview. 29 November 1989.

Clark, Tobin. Telephone interview. 4 January 1990.

Dale, Doris Cruger. "The Learning Resource Center's Role in the Community College System." *College and Research Libraries* 19 (1988): 232–238.

DuCote, Richard. Telephone interview. 12 December 1989.

Gee, Gordon E., and Patricia S. Breivik. "Libraries and Learning." In *Libraries and the Search for Academic Excellence*. Ed. Patricia S. Breivik and Robert Wedgeworth. Metuchen, N.J.: Scarecrow Press, 1988. 25–39.

Hisle, W. Lee. "Libraries in Learning Resources: Has the Cornerstone Become Just Another Block in the Foundation?" In *Academic Libraries: Myths and Realities*. Ed. Suzanne C. Dodson and Gary L. Menges. Chicago: American Library Association, 1984. 378–381.

––––––. Telephone interview. 11 November 1989.

Keough, Lee. "The Persistence of Hypertext." *Computer Decisions* July 1988: 60–63.

Key Charlet. Telephone interview. 14 December 1989.

"Learning Resources Personalities: Ralph G. Steinke." *Community and Junior College Libraries* 6.2 (1989): 30–34.

Lindgren, Bill. Telephone interview. 5 December 1989.

Martin, Susan K. "Information Technology and Libraries: Toward the Year 2000." *College and Research Libraries* 50 (1989): 397–405.

Moore de Diaz, Laurita. Telephone interview. 30 November 1989.

Neill, Gretchen H. Telephone interview. 9 December 1989.

"ON TRACK . . . Information Access Company Databases Debut on CARL System." *ON CARL: The Newsletter of the Colorado Alliance of Research Libraries* (November/December 1989): 9.

Ragan, Lawrence C. "HyperCard—A User's Description." *TechTrends* September 1988: 38–39.

Ray, Donald. "The Meaningful and the Procedural: Dilemmas of the Community College Library." *Journal of Academic Librarianship* 15 (1989): 147–150.

Riggs, Donald D., and Gordon A. Sabine. *Libraries in the Nineties: What the Leaders Expect.* Phoenix: Oryx Press, 1988.

"Standards for Two-Year Community, Junior, and Technical College Learning Resources Programs." *C&RL News* 50 (1989): 757–775.

Steinke, Ralph. Telephone interview. 4 January 1990.

Suarez, Cecilia C. "The Library and the Remedial/Developmental/Compensatory Education: A Case Study." *Library Trends* 33 (1985): 487–499.

Swanson, Barbara. Telephone interview. 12 December 1989.

Terwilliger, Gloria. "Conditions of Success." *Community and Junior College Libraries* 1.1 (1982): 1–2.

Thomas, John B. Telephone interview. 11 December 1989.

Wagner, Colette A., and Augusta S. Kappner. "The Academic Library and the Non-Traditional Students." In *Libraries and the Search for Academic Excellence.* Ed. Patricia S. Breivik and Robert Wedgeworth. Metuchen, N.J.: Scarecrow Press, 1988. 43–56.

Yoshikawa, Viveca. Telephone interview. 27 November 1989.

Standards for community, junior and technical college learning resources programs

The new standards, approved by ACRL and AECT.

These standards apply to two-year or three-year academic institutions awarding an associate degree or certificate. They are intended to assist in evaluating and developing learning resources programs. With approval by the Association for Educational Communications and Technology and the Association of College and Research Libraries, the document replaces "Guidelines for Two-Year College Learning Resources Programs (Revised)" and "Quantitative Standards for Two-Year Learning Resources Programs."

Two-year colleges make a significantly different contribution than other academic institutions. The public institutions, because of community control, are generally more responsive to local needs. Moderate costs and open-access allow greater flexibility to students who would not otherwise be able to attend college. Emphases on vocational and adult programs and continuing education provide employable skills to many adult students through responsiveness to changing vocational needs. At the same time, while allowing for remedial work to remove deficiencies, academic programs in private and community colleges parallel education in the arts and sciences in four-year institutions. Reflecting the combination of availability of opportunity and expectation of excellence in performance, more than half of the students pursuing higher education are enrolled in community, technical and junior colleges nationwide.

The emphasis being made by the American Association of Community and Junior Colleges, especially for community colleges but also applicable to other two-year institutions, upon the building of communities, upon partnerships for learning, and upon excellence in teaching, requires resources and services which must be provided in accordance with these standards if the vision is to become reality. (See American Association of Community and Junior Colleges, *Building communities: A Vision for a New Century,* a report of the Commission on the future of community colleges, 1988.)

In most two-year institutions an expanded concept of learning resources provides services to the college community. The term "learning resources" is applied in these standards to an organizational configuration which provides library and media materials and services. In addition, learning resources programs can provide various specialized services and perform other instructional responsibilities.

The structure and function of a learning resources program in each institution obviously has been determined by the role assigned within the institutional structure. This role must be consistent with the stated mission of the institution. It must also be related realistically to the institution's educational goals, curricula, size and complexity, as well as the diversity of resources needed to accommodate different modes of learning.

As an educational entity, the learning resources program with audiovisual responsibilities must provide the needed services in a technological environment which requires a substantial proportion of the campus budget. The combination of a number of related responsibilities under the title of a learning resources program is an effective and reasonable way to make the maximum use of the budget. This will expand the role and structure of the learning resources center, and, thereby, create an organizational unit which can provide all major instructional requirements needed to support the diverse educational programs.

Contents

Standard One: Objectives

1.0 The college shall develop a comprehensive statement of the mission of the learning resources program based on the nature and purpose of the institution.

Commentary. A clear and unambiguous statement of the role of the learning resources program is essential for accountability, administration, and review regardless of the organizational structure. Where there are public multi-college districts, separate mission statements should be developed for each campus; multi-campus community college districts may either develop mission statements for each campus or prepare a comprehensive statement for the district-wide learning resources program components.

1.1 The mission statement shall be developed by the learning resources staff, in consultation with the widest possible representation of the college community. The statement or statements shall be endorsed by the governing board and shall be reviewed periodically.

Commentary. Assignment of responsibility to the learning resources staff for the development of the statement and for its utilization and review is appropriate.

1.2 The mission statement shall be used, along with institutional educational goals, in the annual planning process.

Commentary. The mission statement serves as a mirror for the evaluation of services and the projection of future needs. As such it becomes an integral part of the planning process.

1.3 All component units of the learning resources program, whether administered centrally or administered by other campus units, should be clearly defined.

Commentary. The learning resources program should include essential and basic library and media services as identified in the lists in Appendices A and B. There must be explicit understanding of the units which comprise the centralized services. The learning resources program may include other special components such as those listed in Appendix C. To standardize statistical data nationally, decentralized service units (those that report to other departments) should provide needed information about staff and expenditures for reporting to external agencies.

1.4 The learning resources program shall be an integral part of the institution's process for the improvement of instruction.

Commentary. An effective learning resources program is and must be immediately and intimately involved in the entire educational program. There must be participation in curriculum development and approval because the identification and acquisition of resources to support any curricular changes requires time for planning services that may be needed, reading lists that could be provided, bibliographical instruction that must be given, and priorities on use of resources that should be established. Introduction of new models of instruction that require student use of self-paced materials and equipment in centrally-administered facilities require lead time for planning equipment acquisition, development of procedures, and preparation of materials and staff.

Standard Two: Organization

2.0 The responsibilities and functions of the component units of the learning resources program within the institutional structure shall be clearly defined.

Commentary. The services provided are directly related to the quality of the educational program. When restricted to only a small number of basic services, the quality of the instructional program is inhibited; when too vaguely defined, valuable resources will be poorly utilized. Clarity in identifying functions and specificity in assigning responsibilities will provide a learning resources program potentially capable of meeting the needs of the college. Institutional manuals, procedures, and job descriptions confirm the status of the program.

2.1 The duties and responsibilities of the chief administrator of the learning resources program shall be clearly defined within the institutional structure.

Commentary. The chief administrator is responsible for administering the program and for providing leadership and direction so that mission of the program is fulfilled. The administrator should report to the chief academic officer and should have the same administrative rank and status as others with similar institution-wide responsibilities; a title such as Dean of Instructional Services or of Learning Resources is appropriate.

2.2 The comprehensive learning resources program shall include a variety of services which are organized into functional units.

Commentary. The type of component units needed and included will vary from institution to institution and campus to campus. Some possibilities are: technical services, library services, media services, learning development, reprographic services, professional materials services, video production, graphics production, learning laboratories, and computer services. A listing of many of these can be found in the Appendices. Services which are not administratively under the supervision of the program's chief should have a secondary relationship to the learning resources program to allow comprehensive planning and reporting and to avoid duplication.

2.3 The administrator and professional staff should be involved in all areas and at all levels of academic activities and institutional planning.

Commentary. The professional staff members should be involved in major college committees and participate in faculty affairs to the same extent as other faculty. The chief administrator must meet regularly with college administrators and department heads and, along with the professional staff members, must be involved in planning, implementing, and evaluating the instructional program of the college.

2.4 Advisory committees should be formed to provide essential information to the staff and to serve as a link with users.

Commentary. Advisory committees are appointed, elected, or selected by the appropriate faculty, staff or student constituencies. The development and evaluation of services can be more effective because of their responses.

2.5 Internal administration of the learning resources program should be based on staff participation in decisions on policies, procedures, and personnel.

Commentary. While the chief administrator is ultimately responsible, the basis for internal administration should be participatory governance through regular staff meetings and internal communication. The administrator is responsible for reporting to the staff on institutional plans, anticipated curriculum changes, and matters affecting the internal effectiveness of the learning resources program; in turn the administrator will report concerns and recommendations of the learning resources staff to the college administrator.

Each professional and supportive staff member must be provided with a position description which clearly identifies the duties and responsibilities of the position and superior and subordinate relationships. Performance appraisal standards must be clearly defined and understood by all staff members. In addition to a general administrative manual, each unit may require a supplementary manual which provides policy and procedural statements, duty assignments, other organizational matters, and items of general information pertaining to its particular unit. Policy and procedures manuals covering internal library governance and operational activities shall be made available to all staff members.

Standard Three: Administration and staff

3.0 Sufficient and qualified professional and support staff should be available to implement the services for which the program is responsible.

Commentary. Table A evaluates the requirements for adequate numbers of staff on a single campus. The figures are for full-time positions at two levels, basic and excellent, based on full-time equivalent student enrollments. The table does not include services listed in Appendix C as peripheral; if any of these services are assigned, additional staff will be needed in addition to the positions in the table. There is a direct relationship between staff, budget, and services. When staff level and funding level increase, the number of services possible will also increase; the reverse is also a dangerous possibility which should be avoided. If enrollment is 50% greater than FTE, additional staff will be needed. Another factor which affects staff requirements is the ratio of total enrollment to full-time equivalent students. The higher the ratio the greater will be the need for additional staff beyond the formulas in Table A. If there is a regular summer session at the college, the positions in Table A should be based on an eleven or twelve month equivalency. If, in a multi-campus or multi-college district, some services are centralized, additional personnel will be needed.

3.1 The chief administrator shall be professionally trained and knowledgeable about all types of library and media materials and services.

Commentary. The training and experience of the chief administrator shall be as a librarian, a media specialist, or an information specialist with cross-training desirable. The minimal professional degree and prerequisite for the position is a master's degree in educational technology or library services. In order to interact with other administrators and the learning resources staff the chief administrator should demonstrate knowledge of effective management. To make decisions on costly new information services, the administrator

TABLE A *

STAFFING REQUIREMENTS FOR SERVICES
(excluding those in Appendix C**) ***

FTE Students	Administrators	Professionals		Technicians		Other Staff****		Total Staff	
	Min. and Excel.	Min.	Excel.	Min.	Excel.	Min.	Excel.	Min.	Excel.
Under 200	1		2	1	2	1	2	3	7
200–1,000	1	2	4	2	4	2	3	7	12
1,000–3,000	1	3	5	3	6	3	6	10	18
3,000–5,000	1	5	7	5	8	4	8	15	24
5,000–7,000	1	7	9	7	12	6	11	21	33
7,000–9,000	1	8	11	9	17	7	14	25	43
9,000–11,000	1	10	15	11	20	9	17	31	53
11,000–13,000	2	14	21	13	24	11	20	40	67
13,000–15,000	2	16	24	16	28	13	24	47	78
15,000–17,000	2	18	27	19	32	16	28	55	89
17,000–19,000	2	20	30	21	36	18	32	61	100

* Does not include student assistants.
** Most will require 3–8 additional positions.
*** Additional staff will be needed if enrollment is 50% greater than FTE.
**** Secretaries, clerks, lab aides, etc.

should have continuous experience with new technologies.

3.2 The professional staff shall have a graduate degree from an accredited institution and shall have faculty status, benefits, and obligations.

Commentary. The complexity of the learning resources program may require considerable differentiated staffing by individuals with widely varied professional education and areas of specialization. All should have the same status and recognition as other instructional faculty; where faculty rank exists they should meet the same requirements for promotion and tenure as the other instructional faculty.

3.3 Professional staff should belong to library, media, and other appropriate associations, and professional development should be encouraged through direct financial support of attendance and participation in those local, state, and national organizations.

Commentary. The mark of a professional is not only performance on the job but also awareness of professional trends and technological developments learned at professional meetings and workshops, and from professional journals.

3.4 Technical and classified personnel should have appropriate specialized training or experience; classification, status, and salary should be equivalent to those provided for other institutional employees with similar qualifications.

Commentary. Requirements for training and experience needed should relate to the duties assigned. The relative importance of each type of skill will vary across organizational levels. Supervisors

should be selected on the basis of knowledge, experience, and human relations skills.

3.5 Student assistants are employed to perform a variety of tasks, but they should not be used in place of full or part-time staff personnel.

Commentary. The tasks performed by student assistants are usually of a routine nature. However, second-year students in some technical programs may bring skills of a more advanced nature which may supplement the skills of the staff. Student assistants are valuable sources of student opinion of services. They should be treated with respect by all other staff, encouraged to work responsibly on a job, and be given training for doing their tasks successfully.

3.6 The changing nature of the learning resources programs and technological changes which impact such programs mandate regular continuing education participation by all persons, professional and staff alike.

Commentary. Duty schedules should be flexible enough for staff to occasionally pursue further training during working hours. The institutional budget should include provision for travel to meetings and conferences, for registration fees, released time for in-service training, and participation in teleconferences.

Standard Four: Budget

4.0 The budget for the learning resources program should be developed within the mission statement as part of the institutional planning process; the annual objectives should be developed by the learning resources staff.

Commentary. The significance of the mission statement and the annual defined objectives forms the basis for the fiscal process for all of the budget except acquisitions. Stable funding for acquisitions based on the collection development policy is necessary for effective service. Unfortunately consistent funding is the element least congenial to the development of annual objectives and is most affected by decreases; care must be taken to provide adequate information about the significance of stability.

4.1 An ample and stable budget should be based either on a percentage of educational and general budget totals for the institution as shown in Table B or on a full-time student equivalent dollar basis as shown in Table C.

Commentary. Basing the learning resources budget totals on a percentage of the educational and general funds is the preferred approach, but, because this percentage represents the final stage in the budget process, it is difficult to determine during the budget planning. Capital funds are not included in the percentage except for acquisition of library materials.

TABLE B *
LEARNING RESOURCES BUDGET AS % OF
EDUCATIONAL & GENERAL EXPENDITURES

Size	Minimum	Excellent
All	6%	9%

* Appendix C activities and services will require additional funding.

An alternative which uses a per full-time student equivalent dollar figure will allow planning of collections and services upon a more stable basis. Table C is based on 1987 dollars; when there is inflation these figures should be adjusted upward accordingly. There is a correlation between services, collection, and staff size and the level expenditures. Neither table includes capital expenditures. Technological changes, automation, replacement of equipment, and other capital expenditures will require additional funds. Neither table involves capitol expenditures except for library materials.

4.2 Local level processes should be developed so that all expenditures other than payroll originate within the learning resources program and all invoices should have the approval of the chief administrator.

Commentary. Management involves full responsibility for expenditures; no payments should be made without such written approval. Cost analyses and financial planning depend upon the control of adequate records, but these are not always the same records needed by the business offices. To

TABLE C *
DOLLAR EXPENDITURE PER FTE STUDENT
FOR LEARNING RESOURCES OTHER THAN
SALARIES

FTE	Minimum	Excellent
Under 200	211	450
200–1,000	225	400
1,000–3,000	190	375
3,000–5,000	190	375
5,000–9,000	190	375
9,000–12,000	200	400
12,000–15,000	210	410
15,000–19,000	220	425

* Appendix C activities and services will require additional funding.

the legal extent possible and to make the greatest financial savings, purchases of materials should be exempt from restrictive annual bidding and should permit online ordering and standing orders for continuations.

4.3 Internal accounts shall be maintained for evaluating the flow of expenditures, monitoring encumbrances, and approving payment of invoices.

Commentary. An accurate account of expenditures in categories that are meaningful is necessary for fiscal accountability, for monitoring status of accounts, for decision making, and for planning.

4.4 The learning resources budget should provide stable funding for contractual services, equipment, and materials replacement (of three to five percent), and for maintenance of automated public and technical services.

Commentary. Many services are based on continuing support. They cannot be interrupted without serious constraint on the ability to perform effectively. The materials in the collection will become stagnant without a three to five percent replacement of older materials each year.

Standard Five: User services

5.0 The learning resources program should provide a variety of services to support and expand the instructional capabilities of the institution.

Commentary. Learning resources exist to facilitate and improve learning by supporting and expanding classroom instruction and to perform the instructional function of teaching students the information-seeking skills for self-directed studies and life-long learning. As an integral part of the total educational program of the institution, learning resources provide classroom instructional as well as support services to students, faculty, and staff. In some institutions regular classroom instruction in media and bibliographic subjects and service to the community are also provided.

The primary purpose of the learning resources program is to promote learning through the academic program of the institution. To do this the program should provide the best possible access to wanted information in printed, media, or electronic format, and have the means for delivering the information to an individual user or distributing it to campus classrooms. Access in the first instance is provided from the institutions own collection of materials, paired with supportive equipment and efficient service delivery systems to ensure that the available physical resources are deployed for the engagement of students with information and ideas. To integrate new resources of information and new instructional technologies into the ever-changing curriculum, access and delivery systems must be extended through such means as cooperative borrowing or renting materials from other institutions, online searching of large databases, and employing the power of electronic transmission. Most, but not all, potential services are listed in the Appendices.

Students should have access to professional assistance at all times the central facility is open as well as access to materials. Faculty members should have access to basic media production assistance and to assistance in research projects.

5.1 Priority should be given to basic services in accordance with the mission statement; when the program includes special service components, additional staff and funding must be provided.

Commentary. Staff and budget must relate to basic services if service goals are to be met. Special services components listed in Appendix C can and do provide significant support to a learning resources program if the institution is able to afford to provide them, but they must be recognized as supplementing, not replacing, basic services. Table D shows basic services in Appendices A and B which budget and available staff make possible.

TABLE D
NUMBER OF POSSIBLE SERVICES *
FROM RANKING OF STAFF AND BUDGET

FTE Students	Minimum	Excellent
Under 200	16	28
200–1,000	19	30
1,000–3,000	22	35
3,000–5,000	26	40
5,000–7,000	30	44
7,000–9,000	34	48
9,000–11,000	37	52
11,000–13,000	40	54
13,000–15,000	43	56
15,000–17,000	45	58
17,000–19,000	47	60

* From services listed in Appendices A and B only.

5.2 The program should seek to enlarge access to the services available at the college and in the community through networking, resource sharing, online information services, and technological advances.

Commentary. Institutional self-sufficiency is no longer possible today; provision must be made to utilize new delivery systems. Timely access is the key to services. Table D provides a basis for evaluating the number of services which realistically can be provided based on the level of funding and staff. New technology and new services should be adopted as they become useful in meeting institutional goals. The administrator should be prepared to bring to the attention of the faculty and administration new information formats and services as they emerge.

5.3 The services provided should meet the instructional and informational needs of students, faculty, staff, and administration, should provide professional assistance in interpretation, and should include provision for students in off-campus locations.

Commentary. Successful performance is indicated when the needs of students are met. Professional staff as part of the instructional faculty must be accessible to students and must help them gain the skills needed to become self-reliant and critical users of information services. Close cooperation with the classroom faculty is mandatory. Off-campus instruction at a multi-use center must be supported by branch services or by contract services with an accessible library in accordance with ACRL's "Guidelines for Extended Campus Library Services."

5.4 Services are provided for all levels of user: students and other members of the college community.

Commentary. The two-year college has a heterogeneous population with widely different needs. Care must be taken that services provided will met the needs of every individual. This means that the gifted and the remedial student, the recent high school graduate and the mature adult, the physically handicapped and the limited English student can each receive the services that individual student requires. Other campus groups have differing research and informational requirements which should be given careful consideration.

5.5 Necessary instructional equipment is available and managed in the most efficient manner to insure effective utilization.

Commentary. Equipment must be available when and where it is needed; some equipment may be kept permanently in appropriate classrooms or where materials are found. Equipment must be maintained in operating condition and should be replaced on a scheduled basis, taking into consideration obsolescence, operating condition, and age. Capital funds should also be available to insure that advantage can be taken of new technological advances.

5.6 Provision should be made for instructional support production services.

Commentary. Production services should consist, at a minimum, of visualization services, such as production of overhead transparencies, and audio services, such as recording of lectures and speeches, and duplication of these. As staff and budget allow additional production capabilities should be added to meet institutional requirements.

5.7 There shall be a program to provide to students bibliographic instruction through a variety of techniques enabling them to become information literate.

Commentary. One responsibility of the learning resources program is to provide instruction in the use of the materials and equipment available. In addition to general orientation programs, bibliographic instruction may use many different methods, including group and individual instruction and even credit courses. Traditional reference services should be geared to the provision of individualized instructional assistance at all open hours. The student should be prepared to use new information resources for a lifetime

Standard Six: Collections

6.0 The learning resources program shall make available an organized collection of materials and diversified forms of information useful in the educational process, including various forms of print and non-print media, computer software, optical storage technologies, and other formats.

Commentary. The college must be prepared to utilize new technologies for securing information as these are developed. All types of materials conveying intellectual content, artistic and literary works, programmed texts and packaged instruction are considered resources of information that may be used as tools of effective teaching and learning along with books, periodicals, newspapers, government documents, and microform equivalents. There is not a substitute for a well-selected, immediately accessible collection.

Media materials, including those locally produced, play a vital role in the instructional program of most two-year colleges. The increasing volume of specialized, high quality information recorded on videotape at relatively low cost gives videocassette formats a leading role in delivering current information across all disciplines. Computer software must be treated as a curricular resource for programmed learning, development of basic skills, creative research activities, and preparation for the job world. Online computer services are increas-

ingly important as information resources along with the CD-ROM laser technologies.

Table E provides collection goals using definitions from the Integrated Postsecondary Education Data System (IPEDS) of the Office of Education. The table combines some of the items which are separately reported in the IPEDS, but otherwise they are consistent with it. Quantities under the various columns can be interchanged according to the mission of the institution. For example, an institution with a very strong music program may need to develop a strong collection of sound recordings or videorecordings much in excess of these quantitative standards but may need less of some other items. The basis for evaluation in such a case would be the total holdings for that size institution.

6.1 A collection development policy statement shall serve as the basis for selection and acquisition of materials.

Commentary. Acquiring materials based on a written policy with clear guidelines for selection is the nature of collection development. The statement should be developed in consultation with instructional faculty, students, and administrators. Although there are many alternative ways of writing a collection development policy, the following essentials should be included:

a. The purpose for which resources are required.

b. The primary clientele who are to be served.

c. The kinds of materials which are to be acquired.

d. The various factors of cost and usability which will be considered in determining acquisition priorities.

e. The procedures for handling new types of materials, such as computer software and videocassettes, in conformance to copyright law.

f. The process for leasing or renting materials not readily available or too expensive to purchase.

g. Any arrangements with other institutions for cooperative collection, production, or distribution activities.

h. A statement in support of intellectual freedom and the Library Bill of Rights.

i. A policy on the acceptance and incorporation of gifts into the holdings which recognizes the inherent processing and storage costs.

6.2 The selection of materials should be coordinated by the professional staff, working closely with the campus community; final management decisions as to the order in which materials are to be purchased and what gifts should be accepted and processed in the responsibility of the chief administrator or designee.

Commentary. Professionally trained librarians and information specialists, because of their knowledge of the collection, are best able to give systematic attention to collection development. The im-

TABLE E
SIZE OF COLLECTION FOR A SINGLE CAMPUS

Minimum Collection

FTE Students	Volumes *	Current Serial Subs.	Video & Film	Other Items **	Total Collection
Under 200	20,000	200	125	1,400	21,725
200–1,000	30,000	230	140	2,500	32,870
1,000–3,000	40,000	300	400	5,100	45,800
3,000–5,000	60,000	500	750	8,000	69,250
5,000–7,000	80,000	700	1,250	10,000	92,550
7,000–9,000	95,000	850	1,600	12,000	109,450
9,000–11,000	110,000	900	1,800	14,800	127,500
11,000-13,000	125,000	1,000	2,000	17,400	145,400
13,000–15,000	140,000	1,200	2,200	19,800	163,200
15,000–17,000	155,000	1,500	2,400	22,000	180,900
17,000–19,000	170,000	1,800	2,600	24,000	198,900

* Does not include microforms; an annual replacement of 3–5% is anticipated.
** Includes microforms, cartographic, graphic, audio, and machine-readable materials.

Excellent Collection

FTE Students	Volumes	Current Serial Subs.	Video & Film	Other Items	Total Collection
Under 200	30,000	350	525	3,400	34,275
200–1,000	45,000	400	560	5,000	50,960
1,000–3,000	60,000	600	800	8,000	69,400
3,000–5,000	85,000	800	1,300	11,600	98,700
5,000–7,000	112,000	1,000	2,250	18,000	124,240
7,000–9,000	136,000	1,200	3,000	21,000	161,200
9,000–11,000	166,000	1,400	3,300	26,000	196,700
11,000-13,000	200,000	1,600	4,000	31,000	236,600
13,000–15,000	240,000	1,800	4,500	36,000	282,300
15,000–17,000	285,000	2,100	5,000	41,000	333,100
17,000–19,000	320,000	2,400	5,600	50,000	378,000

portance of knowledge about existing holdings, identifying weaknesses, and determining what should and can be acquired requires systematic attention of professionals. They should have access to bibliographical tools and reviewing sources for effective collection development.

6.3 The collection shall be of sufficient scope and currency to support the curriculum as well as meet individual information needs of students and faculty.

Commentary. The mission of the college will determine the complexity of the collection but an institutional commitment to excellence should mean building and maintaining collections that adequately support: liberal arts and sciences programs to prepare students fully for transfer to four-year colleges and universities; programs that have specialized accreditation (fields such as nursing, radiologic technology, etc.); vocational and technical programs; special programs for job training, retraining, or upgrading of skills in continuing and community education services; and needed reme-

dial programs for non-traditional or under-prepared learners. Materials must be available to meet term paper assignments and classroom student reports and self-paced learning in a broad spectrum of knowledge.

6.4 Obsolete, worn-out, and inappropriate materials should be removed based on a policy statement.

Commentary. Deselection and weeding on a regular basis is indispensable to a useful collection and should be done systematically. A written policy should govern what should be removed, what should be replaced, and what should be permanently retained. Not only do obsolete and inappropriate materials occupy expensive storage space but they also distract from other current materials containing important information. From three to five percent of the collection should be replaced annually. The condition of the collection should be reviewed regularly and needed repairs should be made.

6.5 The reference collection shall include a

ASSIGNABLE SQUARE FEET (ASF) FOR LEARNING RESOURCES
(Excluding Corridors, Stairs, Rest Rooms, etc.) *

Minimum ASF for Learning Resources Facilities

FTE Students	Stack	Staff	User	Media Production	Viewing, Storage & Other	Total Space	Users Stations
To 200	2,000	890	1,925	3,800	4,561	13,176	70
200–1,000	3,000	1,380	4,125	5,000	7,625	21,130	150
1,000–3,000	4,000	1,800	9,625	8,000	15,285	38,710	350
3,000–5,000	6,000	2,500	14,575	9,500	22,065	54,640	530
5,000–9,000	9,500	3,900	26,474	12,500	35,625	87,500	720
9,000–12,000	10,200	5,300	33,500	13,250	44,445	106,695	960
12,000–15,000	14,000	6,980	43,259	14,000	53,265	131,504	1,200
15,000–19,000	17,000	8,940	51,225	15,000	65,025	157,190	1,520

Excellent ASF for Learning Resources Facilities

FTE Students	Stack	Staff	User	Media Production	Viewing, Storage & Other	Total Space	Users Stations
To 200	3,000	1,380	2,340	4,100	5,020	15,920	85
200–1,000	4,500	2,080	4,800	5,500	8,390	25,270	175
1,000–3,000	6,000	2,920	11,000	8,800	16,820	45,540	400
3,000–5,000	8,500	3,760	16,775	10,450	24,270	63,755	610
5,000–9,000	12,000	6,000	22,825	13,750	39,180	93,765	830
9,000–12,000	17,000	8,100	30,250	14,575	48,890	118,815	1,100
12,000–15,000	24,000	10,200	48,950	15,400	58,590	157,140	1,780
15,000–19,000	29,000	13,280	59,125	16,500	71,530	189,435	2,150

* Based initially on legal formulas for California community colleges; these formulas are based on current enrollment statistics. Since enrollments fluctuate and buildings are planned for long-term usage, these tables were adapted for a range, modified by the provisions in other portions of these standards.

wide selection of standard works, with subject bibliographies and periodical indexes in print and electronic formats.

Commentary. Reference is the core of every learning resources center and the beginning point for research. The reference collection should be of sufficient breadth and depth to serve the research and informational needs of the campus community.

6.6 Materials which document the history of the institution should be available.

Commentary. Each institution should collect all available publications and internal documents relating to the institution itself. These could include publications by the faculty as well as materials relating to the history of the college. If other institutions or libraries are not collecting materials about the history and life of the local community in which the college is located, these could also become part of the materials to be collected.

6.7 Collections should be organized to provide users with full, efficient, and direct access.

Commentary. The choice of a classification system, the type of catalog, and the arrangement of

materials are important decisions. Nationally approved systems (such as LC or Dewey) and formats (such as MARC) should be used. Uniform and multiple access through a public catalog is essential to make available information in all types of formats. The public catalog should include all print and non-print items.

Standard Seven: Facilities

7.0 The learning resources program should provide space for housing collections, for study and research, for public service and staff needs, and for basic production.

Commentary. Flexibility is essential to cope with technological developments. Most services should be housed in a central location managed by the chief administrator. When components are located elsewhere, these should be located for the most efficient and effective access to these services. Facilities must be planned on a long-term basis, including space for an expanding collection, workspace, machines and other equipment, storage, and the needs of users. Space planning must take into account the need for computer workstations, for transmission and retrieval of information by telecommunications, for media production, and for related requirements within the building for electrical and conduit connections. Space needs of basic components require as a minimum the space indicated in Table F. Additional space should be provided when special services (such as are found in Appendix C) are included in the responsibilities of the learning resources program.

7.1 The space for user activities should accommodate a wide variety of learning and study situations, should be attractive, comfortable, designed to encourage use.

Commentary. Proper arrangement and sufficient space for utilization of instructional equipment and materials, for the needs of the physically handicapped, and for both isolated individual study and for conference and group study is essential. Space should also be provided for group bibliographic instruction.

Display and exhibit space, preview space, and study areas for faculty are desirable. With technological developments, planning for use of specialized equipment requires consideration in terms of electrical connections, cables, conduits, lights, environmental control, fire protection, security, and other factors which affect service. The increase in telecommunications may justify cable linkage to faculty offices, classrooms, and to outside locations.

7.2 Space assigned to learning resources should be restricted to the functions for which designed.

Commentary. Space designed for learning resources use should not be filled by other campus activities when these will adversely impact the learning resources program.

Appendix A: Checklist of basic library services and activities

Listed below are specific services which are considered to be normal and basic services in learning resources program budgets in two-year colleges. Inclusion does not mean that an institution must or should have every activity or service listed.

Acquisition of computer software.
Acquisition of microforms.
Acquisition of non-print materials.
Acquisition of print materials.
Automated online catalog.
Bibliographic instruction.
Circulation of print materials.
Circulation of non-print materials.
Collection management.
Computer reference searching.
Government document borrowing.

Government document selective depository.
Independent study guidance.
Institutional publications reference collection.
Instructional television individualized access.
Interlibrary borrowing
Interlibrary lending.
Laser optical/reference searches.
Literacy training materials.
Local history collection.
Machine-assisted cataloging of books.
Machine-assisted cataloging of audiovisuals.
Microcomputers for public use.
Microform cataloging.
Microform print service.
Online public access catalog.
Participation in bibliographic networks.
Physical access to materials.
Preparation of bibliographies.
Processing of audiovisuals.
Processing of microforms.
Processing of print materials.
Reference services.
Reserve book service.
Selection of materials.
Self-service copy machine.
Special collections services.
Telefacsimile service.
Telephone reference service.
Term paper counseling.
Union card catalog.
User-available typewriters.

Appendix B: Checklist of basic instructional media activities and services

Listed below are services which are considered to be normal and basic services in two-year college learning resources program budgets. This list may not include future technologies and services. Inclusion does not mean that an institution should have every activity or service listed.

Adult literacy laboratory.
Audiocassette duplication.
Audiocassette editing.
Audiocassette recording.
Audiovisual equipment maintenance.
Audiovisual equipment distribution.
Closed circuit television.
Copyright consultation.
Darkroom services.
Equipment distribution.
Equipment maintenance.
Equipment repair.
Equipment specifications.
Graphic art layouts.
Group presentations.
Group television viewing.
Identification photography.

Instructional design and development counseling.
Instructional film and video renting and borrowing for classroom use.
Instructional materials scheduling.
Interactive television.
Inventory of audiovisual equipment.
Listening services.
Microcomputer literacy.
Media orientation and instruction.
Motion picture photography.
News photography.
Photography for slides.
Preview services for faculty.
Production of instructional materials.
Production of sound slide programs.
Satellite communication downlink.
Scripting of audiovisual presentations.
Scripting of television modules.
Self-paced learning assistance.
Telecourse availability information.
Television off-air video recording.
Television off-site video recording.
Videotape editing.
Videotape multi-camera production.
Videotape one-camera production.

Appendix C: Checklist of special services components

This list includes technologies and roles which, if assigned to the learning resources program, will require capital funds, space, personnel, and operational budgets in excess of those included in Tables A to F. Inclusion of programs in this list is not advocacy for these services as part of the learning sources program but recognition that some institutions have included them in the supervisory responsibilities of the chief administrator.

Adult literacy program direction.
Auto-tutorial laboratory.
Career counseling.
College catalog production.
College press.
Community cable televised instruction.
Computer center.
Copy shop (not self-service)
Cross-divisional programs.
Government document full depository.
Institutional records center and archives.
Instructional design office.
Library technician curricular program.
Materials preservation laboratory.
Media technician curricular program.
Print shop.
Public library branch services.
Public museum.
Radio on-air broadcasting station.
Records management.
Satellite communications uplink.
Special learning laboratory operation.
Teleconference and distant learning.
Telecourse administration.
Television on-air broadcasting.
Television course broadcast-level production.
Television station maintenance.
Testing.
Text-book rental service.
Tutoring program supervision.   ■■

Reprinted from College & Research Libraries News, *September 1990, a*
publication of the Association of College & Research Libraries,
a division of the American Library Association

ASSOCIATION OF
COLLEGE
& RESEARCH
LIBRARIES

Association of College & Research Libraries
A Division of the American Library Association
50 E. Huron St., Chicago, IL 60611-2795
312-944-6780
Toll free: 1-800-545-2433, ext. 2516
FAX: 312-440-9374

NOTES ON CONTRIBUTORS

Ngozi P. Agbim is Chief Librarian and Professor at LaGuardia Community College of the City University of New York. As Chair of the Library Department, Professor Agbim is also responsible for supervision of Media Services, including a television studio for in-house curriculum materials production. His academic credentials include a B.A. in history, an M.L.S., and an M.A. in sociology.

Ruth Ahl is the Library Director at Waukesha County Technical College in Pewaukee, Wisconsin. She is also WISPALS Coordinator for the Wisconsin PALS Consortium. As Library Director she is responsible for all aspects of the operation of the library including satellite collections. Ms. Ahl received her B.A. from Valparaiso University, Valparaiso, Indiana, and an M.S.L.S. from Drexel University, Philadelphia, Pennsylvania.

Camila A. Alire is Dean of Auraria Library, University of Colorado at Denver. The Auraria Library provides library service to three institutions on one campus: the University, Metropolitan State College of Denver, and the Community College of Denver. Previously, Dr. Alire served as a community college library director for over six years and was an administrator/faculty member at an ALA-accredited library school.

William V. Costanzo received his Ph.D. in English and Comparative Literature from Columbia University. Since 1970, he has taught courses in writing, literature, and film at Westchester Community College in Valhalla, New York. During that time he has written three books and dozens of articles, none of which, he says, could have been accomplished without the warm and skillful support of the college library staff.

Alan Dyment is Dean of Academic Services at Mount Royal College in Calgary, Alberta. His educational background includes the Fellowship of the Library Association (FLA) and an M. Phil. from the University of Wales. In the past, he has been Chairman of the Alberta Council of College Librarians (1976–79) and Chairman of the Community and Technical College Libraries Section of the Canadian Association of College and University Libraries (1982–83).

Alice Beverley Gass is the Director of Learning Resources at Guilford Technical Community College in Jamestown, North Carolina. She has eighteen years' experience in community college learning resources programs. She began her professional career as a librarian following the completion of the Master's in Librarianship from Emory University in 1971. She has earned her Doctorate in Library Science from Columbia University.

Joseph N. Hankin is President of Westchester Community College in Valhalla, New York, and Adjunct Professor in the Department of Higher and Adult Education at Teachers College, Columbia University. He earned his B.A. (1961) from the City College of New York in Social Sciences, his M.A. (1962) from Columbia University in History, and his Ed.D. (1967) from Teachers College, Columbia University in Administration of Higher Education, with a specialization in Community Colleges.

Margaret Holleman is the Director of Library Services, West Campus, Pima Community College in Tucson, Arizona. She earned her M.A. in English from Arizona State University and the M.L.S. from the University of Arizona.

Judy Jorgensen is currently the Associate Dean of Academic Support at Waukesha County Technical College in Pewaukee, Wisconsin. Her responsibilities include adult basic education, high school completion programs, English as a second language, programming for special-needs adult students, minority recruitment and retention, and outreach campuses. Ms. Jorgensen received a B.A. degree from Cornell College,

Mt. Vernon, Iowa, and an M.S. from the University of Wisconsin, Madison.

Antoinette M. Kania is professor and Dean of Libraries at Suffolk Community College, State University of New York, Selden. Over a career of twenty-two years, she has worked as a librarian, department head, director, and dean in community college learning resources centers both in New Jersey and New York. Dr. Kania has an undergraduate degree in Russian from Douglass College, a master's of library science and a doctorate in higher education from Rutgers University. She is an author, lecturer, and consultant on the topic of academic library standards and performance measures and their use in the self-study process.

Gloria B. Meisel is currently an Assistant Professor/Librarian at Westchester Community College in Valhalla, New York, where she coordinates the Bibliographic Instruction program. She has written articles on marketing the BI program and on the importance of bibliographic competencies. In 1987 she was the recipient of the State University of New York Chancellor's Award for Excellence in Librarianship. She is co-chair of the SUNY Library Instruction Committee and is a member of other professional organizations. She is active on campus committees as well, the most recent being the Assessment Committee and the President's Ad Hoc Committee on Women's Educational Opportunity.

Annette Peretz recently retired after more than sixteen years as Director of the Sage Learning Center of the Department of Library/Learning Resources at Bronx Community College in New York. She earned a master's degree in Library and Information Science from St. John's University and a master's degree in Educational Communications from Herbert Lehman College of The City University of New York.

Edwin F. Rivenburgh is Director, Division of Instructional Services at the Community College of the Finger Lakes in Canandaigua, N.Y. He received his B.S. from Syracuse University, an M.S. from Michigan State University, an M.S.L.S. from Simmons College, and a C.A.G.S. from Boston University.

INDEX

ABOUT THE EDITOR

Rosanne Kalick received her B.A. and M.A. from Brooklyn College. She earned her M.L.S. from Pratt Institute. She is Professor and Chairperson of the Learning Resource Center (Library) at Westchester Community College (State University of New York.) Professor Kalick taught high school English prior to becoming a librarian. She has earned the SUNY Chancellor's Award for Excellence in Librarianship and the Medallion Award, Westchester Community College's highest honor, given for her leadership role in developing and expanding library services at the college. Professor Kalick has served on numerous committees and has been an officer in several professional organizations.